Righteous Brood is the b[...] [...]o have when we began our missional journey as a family. It unapologetically unpacks the challenges of family life in today's world and provides a clear, concise, and practical toolkit for any family wanting to join God in his mission in the world.

—BREE MILLS,
mother; coach; speaker; director
and founding partner, Micro Churches Australia; leader,
The Village, Melbourne, a microchurch network church plant

Righteous Brood should be included in every microchurch and traditional church training. Microchurch life is solely based on doing the mission of God as an extended spiritual family, and Hugh has given us a manual and a devotional for how to do it and how not to do it.

—MICHELLE AND ROB WEGNER,
leaders of Kansas City Underground; North American regional director,
NewThing; co-author, *The Starfish and the Spirit*

I have known the Halters for over twenty years, and they are the real deal! They have lived out the principles in this book and as a result have created a family that truly lives on mission. *Righteous Brood* is a must read for any family that desires to have a positive impact, both inside and outside of their home. This book is filled with practical ideas that will help parents foster healthy missional rhythms. The church desperately needs the perspective that *Righteous Brood* gives to those who aim to follow Jesus.

—**DAVE AND LAUREN RUNYON**, co-founder and director
of CityUnite; co-author, *The Art of Neighboring: Building Genuine
Relationships Right Outside Your Door*; parents of four children

Hugh has been a consistent voice in the missional conversation. Not only is he a thought leader, but he's also an amazing practitioner. *Righteous Brood* is an important book that shows us how to have the posture of Jesus, as a family, and be the church where we live, work, learn, and play.

—**BILL COUCHENOUR**, director of deployment,
Exponential Network

Hugh and Cheryl have learned to raise kids by creating a family ethos, where they love their neighbor, exhibit the kingdom, and live in the messiness of life with others. What you hold in your hand is not a prescription for parenting but culture-building principles that steward and disciple young Jesus-people. If parenting is more art than science, then this book gives you the tools, colors, and creativity to begin painting the young canvases you are helping to create.

—**L. ROWLAND SMITH**, national director,
Forge America Mission Network; director, Pando Collective;
author, *Life Out Loud: Joining Jesus Outside the Walls of the Church*;
lead curator, *Red Skies: 10 Essential Conversations
Exploring Our Future as the Church*

This isn't just any old Christian parenting book about how to ensure your kids keep attending church and adhering to certain religious rules. Hugh sees parenting as an invitation to our children to see God's bigger, more breathtaking story and understand their part in it. And it comes from his deeply formed experience. I've known Hugh and Cheryl for a long time. I've met their family. They are indeed a righteous brood.

—**MICHAEL FROST**, missiologist, Morling College, Sydney; author, *Surprise the World*; co-author, *The Shaping of Things to Come*

It has been said that the macrocosm is in the microcosm— that the whole is already present in the parts. What Hugh and Cheryl have modeled and taught for thirty years proves this perfectly. Discipleship starts in the home, and movement happens when our children extend the story they experience in the family! This short, simple book describes the place where we all should start.

—**ALAN AND DEBRA HIRSCH**, authors and long-term practitioners of missional movement; founders and leaders of numerous organizations, including Forge Missional Training Network and Movement Leaders Collective

RIGHTEOUS
BROOD

Righteous Brood

HUGH HALTER

MAKING
THE
MISSION
OF GOD
A FAMILY
STORY

100 MOVEMENTS
PUBLISHING

First published in 2023 by 100 Movements Publishing
www.100Mpublishing.com
Copyright © 2023 by Hugh Halter

The author has no responsibility for the persistence or accuracy of URLs for external or third-party internet websites referred to in this book, and does not guarantee that any content on such websites is, or will remain, accurate or appropriate.

Some names have been changed to protect the privacy of individuals.

Parts of this book originally appeared in a free eBook entitled *A Righteous Brood: Making Your Family the Front Line of Mission*, Missio Publishing, 2012.

All Scripture quotations, unless otherwise indicated, are taken from the NIV, THE HOLY BIBLE, NEW INTERNATIONAL VERSION®, NIV® Copyright © 1973, 1978, 1984, 2011 by Biblica, Inc.® Used by permission. All rights reserved worldwide.

Scripture quotations marked NLT are taken from the *Holy Bible*, New Living Translation, copyright © 1996, 2004, 2015 by Tyndale House Foundation. Used by permission of Tyndale House Publishers, Inc., Carol Stream, Illinois 60188. All rights reserved.

Scripture quotations marked MSG are taken from *THE MESSAGE*, copyright © 1993, 2002, 2018 by Eugene H. Peterson. Used by permission of NavPress. All rights reserved. Represented by Tyndale House Publishers, Inc.

Scripture quotations marked ESV are taken from the ESV® Bible (The Holy Bible, English Standard Version®). ESV® Text Edition: 2016. Copyright © 2001 by Crossway, a publishing ministry of Good News Publishers. The ESV® text has been reproduced in cooperation with and by permission of Good News Publishers. Unauthorized reproduction of this publication is prohibited. All rights reserved.

Scripture quotations marked KJV are taken from the King James Version. Public domain.

ISBN 978-1-955142-29-8 (print)
ISBN 978-1-955142-30-4 (ebook)

Cover design and interior illustration by Revo Creative Ltd

100 Movements Publishing
An imprint of Movement Leaders Collective
Cody, Wyoming

www.movementleaderscollective.com
www.catalysechange.org

CONTENTS

FOREWORD

DAVE AND SUE FERGUSON

We are Hugh Halter fans! He's kind of a mix of your favorite uncle and a slightly cranky, straight-shooter neighbor. He has a big heart and tells things the way they are. And he practices what he preaches.

In this new book, Hugh shares the ways in which he and his wife, Cheryl, have pushed through the hard and challenging seasons of life to not just be hearers of Jesus' commandments to love God and love your neighbor but to be doers, by living it out and investing in the lives of others. As Hugh points out, parents are the ones called to be the main disciple-makers of their kids, and so Hugh and Cheryl invited their kids to come alongside them as they served. They apprenticed their kids in the ways of Jesus, by showing them what it means to love God and love your neighbor in real and tangible ways.

Children are a blessing from God! We truly loved getting to raise our own three. But between school, practice schedules, and music lessons, it was easy to forget that our main purpose in life is to love and serve God and others—not just our kids! If we're not careful, it's easy to make family an idol that takes the place of God and his mission in the world.

Hugh shares some great examples of lessons he and his family have learned—of risks and adventures they took, and continue to take together, as they listened to God's voice and followed. In reading about their faith journey, we believe you will be inspired to go on one of your own. And, as Hugh points out, one of the benefits of this is that your family will draw closer together in the process.

Reading this book made us want to go back and do it all over again, looking for more opportunities to serve Jesus together as a family, having more faith, taking more risks, and being the "righteous brood" God created us to be. If you still have kids at home, seize this book and seize the day—go on a Jesus-following adventure together that you will never, ever regret!

1

COFFEE TIME

Since we were first married, Cheryl and I have tried to have coffee together twice a day. The morning cup is simply for waking up, getting a heads-up on the events of the day, and watching our pets rummage around the yard. The second cup is usually around 4 p.m. It tends to be about recapping the tragedies and triumphs that may have occurred throughout the Halter family that day. Personally, I don't really like the morning cup. I'm an introvert and a bit ogreish when I wake up, so when my extroverted wife wants to break the beautiful silence with a barrage of words, it takes all the discipline in the world to look like I'm into it. Over the years, many of these morning cups have been sipped after only a couple hours of sleep. Our son, Ryan, had acute epilepsy, which meant we could be up most of the night with him. So this cup of dark java was sometimes less about savoring and more about surviving!

These coffees have seen us through raising our three

children—Ryan, McKenna, and Alli—with all the ups and downs of family life, as they went from toddlers, to pre-teens, through to teens and young adults. Over the years, we've planted churches, moved across the country twice, renovated a stack of homes, and settled Ryan into a supported-living facility for disabled adults in Alton, Illinois. The rest of our family eventually ended up moving to Alton with us and have been at the center of one of the craziest city renovation projects I could have ever imagined. And then in 2021, Ryan sadly went home to be with the Lord. (I'll share more about Ryan later.) Through all those changes in our family life, our coffee routine was one of the few constants.

It's always been the afternoon cup of coffee with Cheryl that I look forward to the most. Traditionally, some of our best visions, plans, and creative ideas have come from this hour. Over the years, we've dreamed about vacations, about Ryan getting better, about our girls' hockey tournaments, about my latest book exploits, about our church community, about where I was traveling next, about what our date might be for the week (okay, the month), and a host of other hopeful opportunities.

As I look back, most of those crazy dreams have gone unfulfilled. We were often just stuck in the mundane reality of our children's schedules, financial constraints, balancing ministry and other employment, and of course, Ryan's severe disability.

In the fall of 2011, when Ryan was twenty-four, by sheer

providence, we found the 350-person assisted living ranch for adults with disabilities in Alton. Ryan got accepted into the program and left his ten-by-ten-foot room at home to relocate halfway across the country. Regretfully, he had to leave behind his collection of samurai and William Wallace swords, which meant so much to him. (He actually asked the staff if he could bring along a "few really dull knives." These daggers were four feet long, and even without a sharp edge could do some damage in the hands of an autistic extrovert. The knives stayed behind.)

We were sad that our boy was leaving home. However, because he was so excited, we were also thrilled for him. And, candidly, we were pretty excited for us, too!

As you can imagine, the constant care and trauma of Ryan's decades-long struggle had taken its toll on us. His disabilities kept us from fulfilling more than a few of those afternoon dreams and ambitions. Or at least that's how it felt. Our unpredictable life had also made it almost impossible to take more than a few days off together, and we were only batting about 50 percent on actually getting through a whole date night. Often, we'd have to box up our restaurant food and head home early because Ryan wasn't feeling well.

So, when Ryan's assisted-living plans were finalized, I started dreaming big. I said to Cheryl, "Hey Babe, you and I can take a six-month sabbatical and go on the trip of a lifetime. We'll start off with three weeks at the Tour de France, then Chunnel over to England, then hop up to Scotland for the

British Open. When we get home, I'll start building that log cabin we've always wanted—from scratch!"

Undeterred by Cheryl's furrowed brow and somewhat skeptical look, I continued, "And then you can go skydiving, Rocky Mountain climbing, and even ride a bull named Fumanchu! Whaddya say?"

She clearly wasn't impressed by my ability to quote Tim McGraw lyrics in my plans for our future.

All I heard was a long, drawn-out slurp of vanilla crème coffee. Then, as Cheryl looked over her steaming mug, she said, "You know, before we make all these plans, maybe we should pray about our future."

Without thinking, I blurted out, "No way!" I didn't want God to screw up our only chance at a break, some fun, some frolicking, and lack of responsibility. Cheryl just rolled her eyes while I kept venting. "If we ask his opinion, he'll probably send us to the Congo to start an orphanage or make us go back into youth ministry … or even worse, you'll get pregnant, and we'll have to start all over again!"

Cheryl finally spoke. "You know, I'd love to have an orphanage for all these parentless high school kids who've been hanging around, or maybe we could consider foster care."

Drat! I knew it!

She continued, "I'd love to be able to take a few weeks off and do the Tour de France; that would be a dream come true. But now we have time to really help people. We could move downtown. I could travel with you a bit. Think what God could do with us now!"

As she kept casting an alternate vision for our future, I began to soften. I sensed the beauty of Cheryl's heart. My wife really wanted God to lead in our next season. Our life has been hard, but it's also been an incredible, unfolding story. We've seen God grow our family and so many people around us, and we've even helped build two churches in the midst of the normal grind of real life. Why would I want that to change? I guess I didn't. And I still don't. I want him to keep leading us through the real world. I want our lives to count. I want to know that every day will continue to have sacred moments when God works powerfully through our weaknesses. Yes, I want a log cabin—but even more, I want a real story, a story that will transform our entire family.

RAISING RELIGIOUS KIDS … OR SOMETHING MORE

A few years ago, I dropped off my car at the tire store and walked across the street to what appeared to be a bookstore/coffee shop. With a couple hours to kill, I thought I'd get some writing done. Whenever I walk into a bookstore, I'm curious to see if any of my own books are on the shelves, so before settling down I made my way over to the "church" section. After quite a while looking around, I stood there a little bummed that my books were strangely absent. *Surely they're just sold out*, I thought to myself. So I ventured to the counter and asked the woman there to look up *The Tangible Kingdom*, to see when the next order would be coming in.

"Sir, there's no book listed by that name," she said.

"Hmmm, that's weird. Try *The Tangible Kingdom Primer* or *AND: The Gathered and Scattered Church*."

After a few moments, she uncomfortably said, "Nope, neither of those is listed."

"Sheesh, oh well, must be a computer glitch or something," I replied.

Her look clearly communicated that she thought I was a bit weird. "Is there anything else I can help you with?"

"Well, yeah, how about a cup of coffee?"

This time her response was even stranger. She just stared at me, and then after what seemed like two hours, she gruffly responded, "NO … we don't have that either."

Now I was ticked. It's one thing to hide my darn books from me, but she had a real nerve to withhold my favorite beverage. Even the tire store has coffee!

"Well, do you have anything to drink?" I shot back.

"Yes, we have sugar-free hot chocolate."

"FINE, I guess that will have to do."

With a strong air of tension, I paid the woman and sat down, plugged in my computer, and began to check emails. Within a few moments, three college-age girls came in—bouncy, happy, and chatty. They all took turns ordering chocolate cake, soda pop, and other treats. Just then, I noticed that they all had on the little "Mormon badges." Then it hit me. *This is a Mormon bookstore, knucklehead! Of course they don't have your books. Of course they don't have coffee!*

My curiosity overwhelmed me, and I tapped one of the girls on the shoulder and asked if they'd be willing to answer a few questions. They were very kind, and we saddled up to a round table.

"Okay, so I have some questions about your faith. First, what's with the coffee thing? Why don't you indulge your Starbucks passions?"

"Oh, sir, based on our doctrinal teachings, we don't consume anything that would be addictive."

Jokingly I inquired, "Well, what about the German chocolate cake you're all scarfing down?"

They laughed and said, "Well, so far there's no admonition against chocolate cake, so we're taking advantage of this freedom while we've got it."

We talked a bit more about a host of religious issues, and all three girls were delightfully fun to talk with. As they left, I remember being impressed by their devoutness and their willingness to deny themselves certain pleasures in order to remain faithful to their belief in God. They had what appeared to be a very safe circle of friends in which the peer pressure was toward holiness instead of crazy behavior. Overall, they were the type of kids any parent would be proud of.

Yet, I also felt as if there was something missing from what I hoped my children would become. Did I really want religious kids, or was there something more?

Cheryl and I never wanted our kids to grow up thinking that following Jesus is simply about attending church and adhering to some religious rules. We wanted them to see a bigger story and know that there's an invitation to be part of it.

And that's exactly why I wrote this book. Most of us live in a tension between wanting what seems "good" in the world's eyes and what living as part of God's kingdom really means. We want the "log cabin"—whether that's a forever home in a nice neighborhood, the vacation of a lifetime, or a dream job. And we hope that we can attain those things one day and our faith will fit into that lifestyle without our having to give up anything. The same tension exists when it comes to our kids. If we're honest, do we long for them to live a radical life, sold-out to follow Jesus, or are we more concerned with their achievements, financial security, and moral standing in the community? Maybe all of this seems too far off for you at the moment, and you just want to get through a date night! But my experience has shown me that most of us, as followers of Jesus, want a real story: a story where God does incredible things in our own lives, in our family's life, and in the lives of those around us. And for our kids, that story has to be much bigger than a couple of hours in church on a Sunday.

JESUS STILL SCRATCHES THE ITCH
In March of 2020, every church in America was forced to close its doors, and worshipers could no longer gather in a physical building. Numbers dropped overnight. But even before the

global pandemic hit, America was already losing its worshipers. Every denomination in the country was in sharp decline.¹ Prior to COVID-19, the cracks in the evangelical church were beginning to show, and as I traveled around the country, many churches were begging for help with a reboot or a renewal—or at least some gimmick to stem the tide or delay the death of their congregational movement.

Our kids are growing up in this mass exodus.² As parents, this presents us with a huge challenge. Once upon a time, going to church was the norm—an accepted reality for the average American family. But now our kids are jumping ship as fast as they possibly can. The Sunday-centric, pray-before-meals, don't-do-drugs-and-don't-make-a-baby-out-of-wedlock Christian story isn't big enough to hold our kids' attention.

And it's probably not enough to hold ours either.

Many of our kids see the church's hypocrisy: They see where the money does and doesn't go; they notice the judgment, the double standards, the selective biblical literalism, and the self-righteous stay-safe undercurrents that often accompany normal church life. And they just can't take it anymore. Many of them don't like our political leaders, on either side of the aisle, and they don't trust leaders in general because so many have let them and the world down. They are desperate to discover a transcendent meaning for life, they want to see the world changed for the better, they want to belong in community, and they want a grounded identity with the creator God.

So, how do we engage our children with a bigger story?

First off, consider this: Following Jesus and creating a pattern for your children is not as normal as you might think. Jesus talked about his way being "narrow." What he meant was that his way is not the way of the masses or the way of the religious or what he called the "broad way." His way was a different way that he knew would not be desirable for the general population. Jesus wasn't just talking about a narrow way of morality—his audience were some highly religious people—he was talking about something much more all-encompassing. We can't just be trying to "fit" Jesus into our lives, or add Jesus on at the end of our week. If we do that, you can be sure we'll miss all Jesus calls us to.

And what he calls us to, is to be righteous—or what the Bible describes as "righteous oaks."[3] You might think that means being religious or morally pure or steeped in Bible verses, but it's far different. "Righteous" is a word that describes a unique type of person, one who takes on a sacrificial, servant posture in the world, even disadvantaging themselves for the sake of the larger community. They are the unique few who take their own lives, needs, and wants and lay them down for the sake of others. These righteous oaks are not of the normal cut.

Jesus goes on to call these people his "disciples," and disciples are never just church attenders. Jesus knew millions of religious people would never live sacrificially or show the world his glory, but a handful of narrow-way people would. His movement was to be formed around a countercultural band of righteous revolutionaries who brought mercy, justice, and peace anywhere it didn't exist.

This book is about helping you grow your *righteous brood*—showing you how to nurture a nest full of crazy, unique, powerful, and sacrificial humans who love the world, or at least their little part of the world, and who point people to Jesus the King and his great new kingdom.

Jesus grew a righteous brood by investing in a small band of men and women from all walks of life. And he launched the greatest missionary movement the world has ever seen. And, as we see in the early church of the Epistles, the family home, not just the temple, became the key training ground for discipleship and sharing the gospel.[4] It was no longer just rabbis and religious teachers who were to disciple others, but everyone—including dads and moms. You see, as parents, we are well positioned to be a modeling presence for the next generation to learn about how to live as Jesus-followers. Parents, raising a righteous brood is part of Jesus' plan to see justice, mercy, and the fullness of his kingdom transform the earth. He wants to see you growing your kids into people who will usher in God's kingdom, for the good of all.

Looking further back in our Bibles, the family has always been the front line, the strategy, the witness, and the training ground for God's message to be proclaimed and lived out. From Genesis to Revelation, God's story is one of taking his people—a collective, a community, a family—on an adventure so they might show and tell the world what he is really like, demonstrating his glory. And the call is no different for us today. God is calling us, as families, to this same adventure.

GOD'S GREATER STORY

If you're looking to simply keep your kids in church and ensure that they follow a checklist of Christian rules, this book will disappoint you. Everything I've learned in the last thirty years about raising a family that follows Jesus has shown me that the Christian faith is much more than a moral code or a list of rules to abide by. It's much more than a few hours in a church service. Jesus' invitation to his disciples was to join in with his Father's mission—a mission that is about reaching, changing, and redeeming every part of his world. Right from the fall of Adam and Eve, God's plan has been to redeem and restore all things to himself. The pain and sin of the world was, and is, so bad, that God sent Jesus as a redeemer to disarm sin and start a movement of people who would shrug off the kingdom of darkness and instead work as salt and light to create a city on a hill,[5] full of God's blessing and wholeness. Jesus has called us to participate in that great mission with him. He commissioned his disciples with the words, "As the Father has sent me, I am sending you" (John 20:21). And that commission extends to me and you today, as his disciples. It might cost us everything we have, but it will always be worth it. It will be more satisfying than the log cabin or anything else we may set our hearts on. Being part of this mission as families will mean our kids can experience the joy of seeing God at work firsthand in their own lives and in the lives of those around them. It will help them learn to trust God for themselves. And it will help them form a real relationship with God.

Sadly, for most of us, when we think of being "sent," we think of the missionaries who travel halfway around the world to share the gospel. But being sent was never intended for just a few radical disciples. It certainly wasn't only intended for certain parts of the world, far away from us. Jesus called his disciples to share and live the good news locally, regionally, nationally, and globally (Acts 1:8).

So, it seems that mission is an invitation and expectation for all of us, as individuals and as families. That means that God's mission includes you. You don't have to be a professional saint or perfectly positioned. This missional call has always been given to the common folk: the exhausted priests, the prostitutes, the peasants, and those without status.[6] So whether you're feeling strong or weak, full to the brim or running on empty, God wants you and your family to join with him in his mission. He's just looking for willing hearts. The call to go into the world with the good news of God's favor is for everyone who struggles with human limitations—for those who can't find time to work out or read a book because family life is so crazy-busy; for those whose families are messy and who struggle with their own issues; for those who teeter on the edge financially; for those who parent alone; and for those trying to blend families after difficult divorces and daily drama.

This book is for those who want to live this bigger story

but also live in the reality of everyday life. Believe me, I know what that's like.

For the first six years of Ryan's life, he would average about ten seizures a day. His seizures were called "grand mal"—the big ones that cause sufferers to contort, drool, flop around, and make dreadful noises as they try to breathe, often turning blue from lack of oxygen. Some liken these seizures to wrestling five rounds without a break. After going through this, Ryan would usually wet himself and lie completely limp, unable to move at all.

Early in our marriage I was working as a house painter, and a typical day would go something like this: Two or three hours of sleep because of Ryan's seizures. Coffee first thing. Off to paint at 5:30 a.m. Home by 3:30 p.m. Quick shower. Afternoon coffee. Then, one or two nights a week, we'd either have a community time, Bible study, or I'd head out to spend time with local brothers who were trying to follow Jesus. Then again that night, a few hours of sleep, interrupted every couple of hours by Ryan having a violent seizure. Repeat.

Eventually, after planting our first church, we began to feel a meltdown coming. There were too many dumb church squabbles. I was getting jaded and figured—for legitimate reasons or simple justification—that it was time for the Halters to come off the field of mission, be normal, hide out, and recover. Through all those years, often when circling a mall or going downtown, Cheryl and I would joke about wanting to get ourselves a "handicapped" sticker to make life easier (at least the parking).

Of course, Cheryl was always tougher than me and would just soldier on, but Hugh Halter was done! I wanted to literally hang the handicapped sticker in my car and on my front door, and print a few t-shirts that said, "Leave me alone. Don't ask me to lead anything, do anything, or care about anything ... and that goes for you too, God!"

So, I resigned from my church-planting job. We moved a few hours south of Portland, and I decided our family had done enough for a God who was apparently too busy with world hunger to lend a hand to a faithful servant up in Oregon.

Maybe you're feeling something similar. Maybe you're asking how we—who barely have time to breathe—can open our hearts and homes to the weary and hungry and thirsty.

How can we feed our families—in all the senses of that term—and feed the world, and still get enough downtime to keep us semi-human?

And furthermore, why would we sign up for that added stress?

Our move south of Portland wasn't the end of the story. God showed us how his grace can break through in the broken places of our lives, and it's then that we often observe something of God's kingdom at work. What we learned was there's no better way to experience Jesus' story as real than by getting involved in his mission. It's only when we step out of what's comfortable and normal that we truly experience the life-giving, risk-taking faith that God always intended us to have. Discovering what Jesus meant by "life to the full"

(John 10:10) doesn't happen when we run away, when we retire, or when life feels more manageable. It happens when he meets us in our brokenness as we pursue his bigger story, together.

LIVE A STORY BIG ENOUGH FOR YOUR CHILDREN ... AND THEIR CHILDREN

It might not surprise you to hear that my coffee conversation with Cheryl didn't end with me building a log cabin. I share more of that story later in the book, but needless to say, I remembered that our life wasn't about seeking to fulfill my own needs; it was about seeking God's kingdom impact and transformation on earth. That wasn't about to change just because our kids had left home.

And the exciting thing for us in this later stage of life has been seeing how our girls are living out their own part of God's big story too. (It's also fun that they and their husbands now share some of their coffee times with us.)

What you draw people with is what you draw them to. In other words, if we take our kids to church their whole lives, we'll draw them to be church attenders. But if we draw them to loving Jesus through serving those on the margins, hosting great parties with crazy neighbors, and forming deep community and intentional mission, we'll draw them to a life of doing the same.

Each of us disciple who we are. When Jesus commissioned his disciples toward the end of his earthly life, he instructed them to make disciples and teach them "everything I have commanded you" (Matthew 28:20). The disciples were called to pass on the life that Jesus had imparted to them. When Paul said to his followers, "Follow my example, as I follow the example of Christ" (1 Corinthians 11:1), he was likewise calling his disciples into the life he had modeled. If we are willing to risk all and live a story that keeps our children's attention and respect, they will most likely follow in it. What else would they do? Settle for church attendance? What if our kids were so enamored with the visible life of Jesus that they would never dream of living any other life? What if the good news of God's kingdom became the petri dish they learned all of life's lessons from? What if you didn't just spend eighteen years passing on a few Bible stories or verses to your kids, but instead found yourself growing them into a righteous brood?

As I look back over the years, I hope that one thing Cheryl and I modeled to our kids was a life of welcoming others into our family, of opening up our home and our lives to those around us. Our kids saw us exhausted but still opening our door. They saw us working normal jobs but still leading a spiritual community. They saw us able to be present at home but still passionate about seeing the kingdom come in the world. They saw us struggle over how to pay our bills but still be generous to those whose troubles trumped ours.

Though we got plenty wrong, what our kids never saw was religiosity, self-righteousness, judgment, or Sunday-centric consumer Christianity. Alli and McKenna are now making the mission of God part of their own families' stories. It's an incredible thing for Cheryl and me to see.

This book is an invitation to discover how you too can make the mission of God a family story—a story that will not only transform the lives of those around you but will also transform your own life, your kids' lives, and even your grandchildren's lives. It's not an invitation made only to those who have life figured out. It's certainly not a guarantee that life will be easier or more comfortable. And, to be brutally honest, it doesn't even come with a guarantee that your kids will go to church or be Jesus-followers in the future. But it is an invitation to the kind of life that will allow them, and you, the opportunity to really know the Jesus who came to save the world—and to join in with the amazing kingdom work he's continuing to do.

IN SUMMARY

- If we're honest, we often long for a "log cabin" rather than God's plans for our lives, but God has a much bigger story for us to be part of.

- We can raise kids who are religious, or we can strive to raise kids who learn to truly follow Jesus.

- When we look at how Jesus started his movement, the home was the training ground, where moms and dads could be part of discipling the next generation.

- God's story has always been much bigger than following a moral code. He is restoring all things to himself, and Jesus has called us, as families, to participate in that great mission with him.

- When we live into God's bigger story and get involved in his mission, our kids can experience what it really means to follow Jesus—and they often end up living their own big stories, too.

SOMETHING TO THINK ABOUT

- What are we longing for or waiting for that means we're missing the invitation to be part of God's bigger story?

- What's our ultimate goal for our kids and their faith?

- Have you discounted yourself and your family from being sent? If so, why is that?

MAKE IT HAPPEN

- Ask God to give you a fresh vision for your family.

- Take some time to repent of any unhelpful mindsets (e.g., longing for a "log cabin" or thinking your family situation disqualifies you from the call to mission).

- Ask God to give you faith for stepping out into something new and raising a righteous brood.

2

THE LURE OF METROVILLE

It was after curfew at Bethlehem Bible College. I was on the campus with a small band of men, including an ex-pro lacrosse player and a world-renowned musician—both a decade younger than me. Every night I had learned to expect them to plan a physical attack on me. I think they liked beating up the ol' man. The problem with their plan, however, was that I was holding my own. On this night, I was tired and warned them that if an attack occurred, I would have to unleash the torrents of hell upon them, and I turned over to go to sleep. Against all wisdom, rock star Brad jumped me! I quickly turned, threw him against the wall, most likely waking up everyone in the West Bank, and proceeded to pummel him. I had him wedged on his bed, and between gasps for air, he blurted out, "Get off me, Bob Parr!"

"What?" I said. "Who the heck is Bob Parr?"

Then, for the next few hours, we talked about Bob ... you know, the father in the 2004 animated masterpiece *The Incredibles.* They said I looked like him—sort of bulking with a sturdy upper frame, large arms, beer gut, and pigeon legs. Well, after that I was actually quite proud, because I thought the movie was epic!

If you haven't seen it, *The Incredibles* is a story about some washed-up superheroes who, by government mandate, are forced to give up their adventurous existence, hide their identities, and adopt a mundane suburban life. Bob, who when on top of his game was beloved by the people and feared by the villains, settles into a job as an insurance salesman. His wife, Helen (aka Elastigirl), who also used to live the wild life of a hero, becomes content to keep house and prevent Bob from trying to relive the glory days. She has her hands full, however, because their three kids—Violet, Dash, and Jack-Jack—were all born with superpowers and are itching to find a positive outlet for their unique gifts.

Eventually, due to the evil villains who keep trying to destroy the world and create global chaos, the Parrs not only come out of retirement but also learn how to be a family on a shared mission. Some days they act like normal citizens, but then, without much warning, they are thrust into superhero mode. The parents, as well as the children, grapple with this strange paradox together, learning to use their unique gifts, and eventually enjoy a sense of victory over the dark forces that target them and the innocent residents of the city.

The Parrs exchanged their somewhat boring existence for a life of adventure, a life that transformed the lives of those around them. Sure, they had to deal with constant tension, but that tension birthed some pretty amazing results. Their lives individually—but even more, as a family—were incredible!

I know it's a movie, but you have to admit it serves as a pretty fair metaphor for the opportunity every family has before them. No, I'm not suggesting that out-of-shape guys put on red leotards, black boots, and a cape, and ask their kids to follow suit; but the story of our faith is a saga of normal people, often in family groups, leaving a mundane life, finding their unique gifts, and advancing together into the adventure and call of the mission of God. It's the story of the Christian faith … at least it was back in the day.

Take Abraham, for example. His was the first missional family. God asked Abraham to leave his country and head out on an unknown mission of becoming the family through whom the entire world would be blessed.[1] Now that's a mission that will keep you up at night! Abraham could have chosen the safe and easy option. He could have stuck with what he knew. But instead, he chose to leave his homeland, trusting God for both himself and his family, and lived a bigger story … one that eventually led to the birth of Jesus.[2]

Theologically, we know we are supposed to be on mission for God, right? The church is called to leave what's comfortable and propel itself out into the darkness as light … into the decay of real life as salt; that its people are to live as aliens and

strangers, adopting the countercultural life of the kingdom of
God.

I think somewhere between then and now, we lost the
story. Or at least we lost how the story came to us. It was the
same in the Old Testament—God was continually sending
prophets to tell his people that they had forgotten their story.
Forgotten where he'd called them from. Forgotten who he'd
called them to be. As twenty-first-century Westerners, we
live independent, individualized, self-contained lives. But the
stories and events in the Bible occurred in a Middle Eastern
context, which tended to value the collective more than the
individual.[3] Middle Eastern ways of life were based on family,
lineage, and passing down the story to the next generation.
When you read stories in the Gospels where Jesus talks to one
person and then he or she goes and tells the whole village,
this was typical of a Middle Eastern way of life. The family
mattered, and God's primary means of extending the gospel
and his reign was through the family—both the nuclear family
(father/mother/children) and also the extended family line
(aunts/uncles/grandparents/cousins). This could also include
friends who needed a place to stay, or workers in the family
business who had become a part of the household.

Now I'm not saying we need to deny our twenty-first-
century Western context. I'm not asking you to trade in
your minivan for a bunch of camels. I'm not going to ask
you to give up electricity, remove your kids from the soccer
club, or suggest you turn your basketball court into a wheat

field. The world has indeed changed—but God's plan hasn't. Yes, I do believe today's world is more complicated. We have more options, more angles of diversion, and more confusion over what it really means to have a Christian family. And the whole definition of family within the wider context of Western society has dramatically shifted over recent years. But whatever the shape or size of your family, trust me, God knows the pressures you are up against. And he also holds the power to transform and reengineer a family around his design of being on the front edge of mission.

Your heavenly Father is super. His Son is spectacularly super, and the Spirit that indwelled him is extraordinary. Ephesians 1:18–21 says:

> *I pray that the eyes of your heart may be enlightened in order that you may know the hope to which he has called you, the riches of his glorious inheritance in his holy people, and his incomparably great power for us who believe. That power is the same as the mighty strength he exerted when he raised Christ from the dead and seated him at his right hand in the heavenly realms, far above all rule and authority, power and dominion, and every name that is invoked, not only in the present age but also in the one to come.*

This means that you have a lot more resources at your disposal than you think you do! Mundane daily struggles you can count on, but God has a way of pulling the miraculous out of it all. It may not always feel like it, but his life and calling for your entire brood can emerge from the rubble of routine.

MOVING IN OR OUT OF METROVILLE

Before we start the adventure, we need to look down and take note of the *terra firma* we live on: the good old-fashioned American-Dream world. For the Parr family, that location was a place called Metroville. Parr for their course and par for us. It's a quiet, normal suburb with all the accoutrements of a missionless life. It represents safety; the children go to school, leave home, find jobs, and then repeat the cycle over and over again, with no pizzazz. There's no overarching goal in life, other than to be happy. There's no substantial reason to be moral, to be different, to be inspirational. It's just one twenty-four-hour day after another twenty-four-hour day. Nothing mystical, nothing adventurous, nothing lost, nothing gained. Maybe it sounds a little like your life?

Perhaps, in the aftermath of COVID-19, some of us are clinging more tightly to comfort, security, and even the mundane, than ever before. Perhaps the period of forced isolation has rewired us to be more inward-focused and more nuclear-family focused. It may feel more difficult than ever to look beyond ourselves. Legitimate pressures of job security, health, and the emotional and mental issues within our own families can make us feel like we haven't got the capacity to look beyond ourselves and our own needs. But when we get trapped in this way of thinking, we close ourselves off from the life God intended us to live.

The world around us is a scary place. But if you're constantly trying to build an iron gate around your kids to keep bad things from happening, eventually you'll have to let them outside the cloistered walls, and they won't be equipped to know God's voice or follow under pressure. Though everything within us may want to batten down the hatches and insulate our kids from all the dangers around us, let's not forget that the classic American life is not without its own, more subtle dangers. Here are some of the ones you really want your kids to avoid:

- Growing up without understanding God's vision for their lives.
- Falling short of their God-given talents and calling.
- Living in fear of what others think of them.
- Living a mundane, joyless life.
- Settling for an unfulfilling job, loser spouse, or licentious lover.
- Choosing the safe option and missing out on seeing the power of God.
- Chasing money and worldly prestige and success.

Metroville represents the kingdom of this world. Although it doesn't look dangerous, we all know it is. Jesus made some pretty harsh comments about the stark difference between his world and our world: "You cannot serve both God and money"

(Matthew 6:24); "Do not store up for yourselves treasures on earth, where moths and vermin destroy" (Matthew 6:19); "Whoever is not with me is against me" (Matthew 12:30); "Do not love the world or anything in the world" (1 John 2:15).

Let's take a look at three of the biggest idols in the kingdom of this world and the impact they have on us as families and our call to live out God's mission. I'll let you know right off the bat, I think these three, although substantial in how they make us think and act, ultimately are mirages. In other words, they present on the surface as ways for us to find happiness, but they won't ever satisfy. As we define them, you may quickly identify with their positive aspects in some sense, but all of them are lies, and none of them really deliver what we think they will. And the worst part of living into these lies is that it limits the adventure, the creativity, and the story our lives will eventually tell.

Individualism

Individualism is the habit or principle of being independent and self-reliant. In social theory, individualism is a way of life that favors freedom of action over any form of collective controls. On the surface, individualism appears to be far better than communism or a society in which there is no personal freedom. But don't be fooled: Individualism presents a truckload of trouble for the missional family. You see, God's mission isn't a personal game. In the Gospels and the early church, life in Jesus was always about the family, the community, and even the nation. As the church formed, God was building a brand-new family ... not a religion, a family. As I mentioned in chapter one, Jesus taught about the new kingdom family and how it was more important than even one's blood family. He said, "My mother and brothers are the ones who hear and do God's Word. Obedience is thicker than blood" (Luke 8:21 MSG).

All this can go against the grain—even for us, as Christians. As a parent, it's normal to want to prioritize our kids. But sometimes we put the individual needs of our kids above God's call to us as a family on mission. We make sure they get the best education we can offer them. We pay for all their extra-curricular activities, and we keep them busy with after-school life and summer camps. We often barely even have a social life ourselves, using our kids' schedules and their personal growth as a justification to keep the treadmill running. But if we're not careful, we can actually make an idol out of our children's extra-curricular lives. We start to believe the lie that we can find happiness and give happiness to our children by fostering their personal development. But by focusing on the individual needs of our kids, we start to miss out on the fullness of life God intended us to have as nuclear and extended families. We're so caught up with putting our kids at the center that we miss out on the blessing of serving others together.

What's more, we bring our kids up to think that the world revolves around them. We can end up feeding the belief that they should be in charge of their own lives, making decisions that firstly benefit themselves and celebrating the things they've achieved in their own strength. They end up with no concept of how their decisions might affect others, and they can miss the joy of shared goals and pursuits. Though it's often a good thing to develop our skills and to celebrate achievements, there's a subtle danger when that starts to draw us away from the call Jesus gives to his followers, which is to "deny [your]selves and take up [your] cross and follow me" (Matthew 16:24). If we bring our kids up to believe that the betterment of their "self" is the highest priority, it's pretty hard for them to learn how to live as servant-hearted followers of Jesus.

Consumerism

Whereas individualism tells us the lie that we'll be better by ourselves or just with our family, consumerism tells us the lie that we'll be happiest if we consume the best (or most tailored to our needs) products and services. Let me illustrate it this way. As I mentioned in chapter one, when Ryan moved to Alton, the rest of our family eventually decided God was calling us to follow him, and we ended up planting a faith community in that town. Amazingly, we were given an incredible space, albeit at the time it was an abandoned building.* We eventually renovated it into a coffee shop, with the vision to create a

---

* There isn't space to share here about the story of us being given Post Commons (the old post office building in Alton) and renovating it into this space for the town, but suffice to say, it was pretty incredible and a real gift from God. You can read more about it on page 54 and on the "About the Author" page.

"living room" space for the people of the town. So now I'm the owner of a coffee shop in Alton, and as part of my job I have to make decisions about products and offers and the vibe we have in the shop because I know if it isn't good, the customers could pick some other place to go, and we would lose sales. The customers, of course, expect to be satisfied, and if their experience doesn't meet the mark, they feel justified in never returning or in posting a nasty Yelp review.

At a business level, it makes sense to pay attention to consumerism, but oftentimes Christians live their entire lives at this level—hopping from one church to another, moving into nicer neighborhoods, or choosing schools that are a thirty-minute drive away because they have better college entrance numbers. Over time, a sinister way of thinking occurs in all of us that makes us feel entitled and deserving of the best of the best, no matter what the cost. As you can see, this is another insatiable lie. The reality is that when God gives us the privilege of raising our righteous brood, we must teach them that it's not about them anymore and that following Jesus is a descending pathway, not an upwardly mobile one. Sure, some of our kids will be financially successful, and this can be fantastic—but only if their success flows from their posture of servanthood to the world they live in.

We need to be conscious of how our identities can be subtly shaped by the consumer choices we make. When we allow our kids to be influenced by a consumer mindset, we risk them placing too much importance on indulging their own preferences and finding their sense of security and identity in the wrong things. When we have a consumer mindset, we start to believe that everything in life is for our benefit, to serve us. This widespread consumer mindset has seeped into the church with toxic results; rather than thinking about who we can serve in our community, we tend to think about what "church" can do for us.

Materialism

Materialism is the last of the big three lies that will not deliver for you or your kids. Materialism is the chasing of possessions and physical comfort as the highest pursuits of our lives. Having material possessions isn't bad in itself; the problem comes when we begin to orientate our lives around the pursuit and gain of material things and the comforts that come with them. This is a serious issue when it starts to get in the way of us following Jesus. It's hard to be obedient to God's requirement to care for the needs of others when we're intent on saving the deposit for that nicer car we've got our eye on. We're great at justifying why we need stuff, and it's usually about our comfort. That's why things like the "wellness" industry are booming—it's all about us spending money in an attempt to feel happy.[4] Interestingly, the opposite of "material" is "spiritual." Jesus' offer of rebirth, and all the benefits of his kingdom, were spiritual, so much so that he constantly urged us to avoid what the world offers— "the lust of the eyes, and the pride of life" (1 John 2:16). Later he taught that we shouldn't even worry about our material body in the unlikely event that someone wanted to put an end to our physical self. In that sense, he said, "Relax, they may be able to kill your body but not your soul" (Matthew 10:28, my phrasing).

This is why we call Christian growth "spiritual growth," instead of calling it "material growth." Materialism can numb our kids from the awareness of needing to grow spiritually.

Whereas in the past our identity was shaped by our family origin, relational ties, and social friendships, materialism encourages us to find identity and express ourselves through the products we buy.[5] This isn't just about stuff; it's about defining who we are in terms of the lifestyle we live. For example, we get our sense of "who we are" from the neighborhood we live in, the job title we have, the school our kids go to, the sports or music lessons they pursue, or the clothing brands we wear. This can even happen in the positive choices we make—the food we eat being particularly healthy, organic, or locally grown; the eco products we use or the hybrid car we drive. We need to be conscious of how our identities can be subtly shaped by the pull to materialism.

How much of your time is spent worrying about whether your kids are looking presentable, or arguing with them about having the latest tech? How many hours have you spent Christmas or birthday shopping for toys, only to be donating them to Goodwill six months later? Many of us have spent way more time dealing with those issues in our kids' lives than thinking and praying about their walk with Jesus. Our primary job is to form them spiritually. If we do that, then no matter their worldly wealth or possessions, they'll be rich in the things that bring the most joy.

THE WEIRD WAY

Yes, I guess you can now say to your kids, "The way of Jesus is weird, and most won't choose it, but it's their loss and our gain." Jesus' own words and the words of his followers make it pretty clear that God's ways are not our ways. And the ways of the world are under the swirling control of Satan and his minions that spin the globe, sucking people into busyness, financial debt, relational strife, vice, depression, and a host of life habits you'd face down a charging lion to keep your kids away from. The bummer is that none of this looks like a predator trying to rip life from you and your children. It looks like the American Dream and is guised in empty promises that seem to trip and snag most of us.

So what do we really want for our kids? How are we aligning our priorities with God's way rather than the ways of Satan and his worldly idols? If we think about prayer, for example, what do our prayers say about the kind of life we want for our kids? And do our actions match our prayers? We all know that we should pray for our kids, but think about *how* you pray for them. My guess is that 99 percent of what you've prayed for has been about their protection from harm, sickness, or pain. There's nothing wrong with that, but by now you've probably realized that our prayers must be far more risky and far more focused on letting God prepare them to be stout-hearted world-changers. Jesus prayed for his closest family and friends that God would not "take them out of the world but that [he] protect them from the evil one" (John 17:15), yet he knew that nearly all of them would die for him.

Do our prayers reflect our willingness to let God take our kids anywhere to do anything at any cost? If not, we need to ask God for courage to pray as we should. Prayer is powerful, and if you really relinquish your children to God's purposes, it may feel like you are risking everything! And if we believe in intercessory prayer, then we're offering ourselves to be used as part of the answer to the prayers we pray.

Cheryl and I have lived with all the pressures and fears many of you will experience. Over the years, the temptation to trade in our divine capes for Metroville's risk-averse ethos has been put before us constantly. We've had to pray hard—often in repentance, as well as in seeking God's wisdom and courage. We know that the lure of Metroville will always be a constant pressure—a pressure that we want to endure ourselves and help our kids learn to withstand as well. What we've found is that the only way to architect a larger story over our families has been to be clear on the bigger and better story: the beauty of God's mission.

IN SUMMARY

- The story of our faith is about responding to the adventure and call of the mission of God.

- Family matters to God, and throughout the biblical narrative, family is God's primary means of extending his reign.

- We have a choice between moving in or out of Metroville. We can choose whether to cling to the kingdom of this world or to move into living the adventure of the kingdom of God.

- Individualism, consumerism, and materialism are three idols of the kingdom of this world that stop us from living as a missional family. They distract and numb us from the spiritual and missional life Jesus is calling us to.

- Our primary job is to form our kids spiritually, but we often spend more time forging a life for our kids that revolves around these three idols.

- Our prayers often reveal something of our priorities and heart for how we want our kids to grow.

SOMETHING TO THINK ABOUT

- What aspects of our cultural context affect how you view following Jesus?

  o Individualism

  o Consumerism

  o Materialism

- How might your prayers change to reflect a desire to follow Jesus and his weird way?

MAKE IT HAPPEN

- Spend some time reflecting on how you make decisions and prioritize your resources as a family or household.

  o How have you previously made decisions about where you live, what activities you and your kids are involved in, and who you are friends with?

  o How do you spend most of your time?

  o How do you prioritize what you spend your money on?

- Consider whether these things reflect more of a Metroville or a kingdom way of living.

- What changes might you make to orientate your family to a kingdom way of living?

3

THE UPSIDE-DOWN KINGDOM

Several weeks after 9/11, I flew on the very first flight after LaGuardia airport reopened. I made my way into Queens and met up with a team of friends that were helping us train church leaders. Being Irish, I had scouted out a nice Irish pub for after our first day of training. When we sat down, a waitress named Fiona served me and my three mates. After the normal food and drink orders, she asked why we had come to town. Not really wanting to talk about God anymore, I deflected, "We're just here training leaders."

Quickly and curiously, she replied, "Oh, great! What type of leaders?"

Still trying not to "go there," I said, "Nonprofit leaders ... you know, folks who are trying to help things out in the city." I hoped that would end the conversation, and we could get back to our holy merriment.

But she pressed, "Wow! That's great. What type of nonprofit leaders are you working with?"

By this point I had lost all creativity, so I confessed, "Actually, Fiona, we're here training young pastors how to start brand new churches."

Like a dark afternoon sky rolling in right before a tornado, her entire face dropped, and she looked puzzled … almost angry. And then came the response that changed my life.

"So why would you want to start more churches if you're trying to help our city?"

We all sat there, with our collective answer somehow suspended in thin air. I remember thinking, *Well, Bible verses ain't going to work here.* And so I asked her a question. "Fiona, did something bad happen to you related to church, Christianity, or Christians?"

She began to share with us some horrific personal stories of being abused in the Catholic school she grew up in and then added a litany of generally lousy experiences she'd had with religion, religious people, and all things churchy.

I was dead in the water. No easy answers would work. And for sure, it wasn't the right time to ask if she wanted us to pray for her.

But then—like the dark clouds moving out and sunlight peeking through a light drizzle, foreshadowing better skies to come—I started talking about things I literally had never talked about in thirty years of pastoral work. What came out of my mouth was about the kingdom of God. And it sounded something like this:

"Fiona, first, thanks for sharing your pain. We are all very sorry that happened, and I can totally understand why you would never want more religious activity to come to your city. But I do know one thing for sure: Jesus hates all that stuff way more than we do, and he hates the stuff that hurt you personally."

Her expression began to soften, and she asked another question. "So then, what was Jesus on about if he didn't want all these churches and religious garbage?"

"Well, Jesus came to earth to give us an alternative to religion, and he called it the kingdom of God. Other times he called it the kingdom of heaven, and I think he called it that because it was the opportunity to reestablish life on earth like it is in the heavenly realm, or even the earthly realm before sin screwed everything up."

Still interested, she asked, "Can you give me a practical example of what the kingdom of heaven might be like here in this dump?"

"Yeah, I can. Jesus said the kingdom is like a mustard seed, which is so small you can barely see it, but it grows into a huge tree. He taught that if we had even a mustard seed's amount of faith, we could see mountains moved. In this neighborhood, how many people do you think are in severe poverty or in an abusive home?" I asked.

"Many," she said.

"Well, what Jesus was saying was that if even one abusive father has a spiritual rebirth and then lives his life after the way of Jesus, the abuse would stop in that family, and it would literally change the legacy of generations in that family. The same would be true with poverty. The moment we help one person escape extreme hunger, or we help pay their rent and keep them off the streets, we are bringing a little slice of heaven to earth. Because, in heaven, there's no abuse, no poverty, no pain, no suffering, no loneliness, no racism, no exploitation, no crime, no vomit on the sidewalk … and all the toilets flush. So, Jesus was inviting us into a life where we bring heaven to earth, even if it's in small doses. And as we do that, the world changes for people."

"I like that," she replied thoughtfully.

The next night, we went back and talked a bit more about the kingdom. On the final night, after all my friends had flown home, I went back at midnight, just to say goodbye to her and wish her well. As I entered the packed pub, I heard Fiona's voice over the crowd. "Hey, that's the guy I was telling you about. You've got to hear how he talks about God." And with that, the crowd split, and she invited me to the bar. "Hugh, I've got to work," she said, "but these are my best friends. Can you please tell them that stuff you were telling me about the kingdom of heaven?"

And so I did.

From then until 5 a.m., I heard why they all quit believing

in church, and why Christians were of no use to them. But every one of them commented that they'd never heard of anything as good as the kingdom of heaven and hoped that someday they would believe that it was real.

And with that, my life changed. I realized that although religion is dying a fast and deserved death, people are still fascinated by Jesus, and love the thought of an alternative way of life where the heavenly way can touch down on planet Earth. In other words, people everywhere are desperate for the gospel … the fantastic news of God's kingdom now!

GOOD NEWS FOR THE WORLD STARTS WITH GOOD NEWSING YOUR FAMILY

I share that anecdote because the gospel is central to the story of a family on mission. It's one thing to go on mission together, but it's far more important to know *why* we are going on mission together. If we're not really sure that the gospel is good news, we're unlikely to feel compelled to share it with others. And, just like the Fiona story, it's got to be good news both in word and deed. Becoming a missional family is really about showing and telling our friends what we've experienced in our home.

If you've grown up in America, and in the normal Christian bubble, the "churchy" gospel fits nice and tidy within our Metroville life. We've been led to believe that the gospel is for after this life, and thus being a good Christian family, or being good Christian parents, is about avoiding sin, exposing our kids to godly wisdom, helping them live a safe and successful life, steeling them against the evils of the world, and then waiting until God comes back to give us the big payoff in the end. This is a generalized version—but if we're honest, it's what many of us have been taught and have lived.

But when Jesus started his ministry, he began preaching for people to repent, or switch their entire life around, because, as he said, "The kingdom of God has come near" (Mark 1:15). In other words, that eternal life was available *now*! It's a bit like a king leaving the throne, walking down amidst all the peasants, and saying, "Look, the way I live up there behind all the high walls is now going to be made available to you normal people down here in the muddy, cold streets." To live into that eternal life means turning away from the kingdom of this world and moving toward the King and his kingdom.

And as Jesus tried to help people learn about the good news (gospel) of this new kingdom, he helped them see the specifics of *why* it was good news. In Luke 4:18–19, Jesus said, "The Spirit of the Lord is on me, because he has anointed me to proclaim good news to the poor. He has sent me to proclaim freedom for the prisoners and recovery of sight for the blind, to set the oppressed free, to proclaim the year of the Lord's favor."

This is why the gospel is such good news. It means that real life will change for people. The kingdom of God is not a place we go after we die but, in Jesus, has come near. The good news is that Jesus has defeated death, that he's dealt with our corruption and sin, and that he's conquered it with his life and with his love. As his followers, we get to experience that for ourselves.

This means our kids can grow up secure in the knowledge that they are loved by their heavenly Father, and there is nothing they can do or say that can make him love them more or less. It means our families do not have to be bound up by the rat race of Metroville, with its pseudo-perfection and pressure to perform. We no longer need to be imprisoned by the way others might perceive us on social media. We do not need to feel anxious about our kids' grades, or the friends they are, or aren't, making. We have been liberated, and we are invited to share that liberation with others—to show and tell about this kingdom.[1]

According to Jesus, his eternal, abundant life is restored and renewed here on earth, and most importantly he said we don't have to wait for it—we can simply recognize that it's already at hand. This is why he taught us to pray, "Our Father in heaven, hallowed be your name, your kingdom come, your will be done, on earth as it is in heaven" (Matthew 6:9–10). So, because in heaven there's no loneliness, pain, suffering, poverty, abuse, judgment, rage, racism, exploitation, greed, crime, and hundreds of other harsh aspects of life, we can begin to pray that those things are eliminated from our lives and the lives of those around us. And whenever we work against these ills and work toward the goodness of the kingdom in its fullest sense, we are bringing heaven to earth; and that is the good, great news, or what we call the gospel! (So even fixing a clogged toilet counts!)

That's the mission of "missional." That's why it's worth taking missional living seriously and why it's worth the potential risks to the security and safety of our family. The gospel (the good news of God's redemptive kingdom now) is the hope of the world; it's the plumb line by which we should measure the worth of our lives; it's the only reason any person would be inspired to persevere, to go against the grain, to be willing to lay aside their own selfish motives.

Okay, so let me say something right now that I've been patiently waiting to tell you. This will initially sound wrong, but it's not, and you must understand it if your offspring are going to be able to influence people spiritually. Here's the statement: The gospel isn't simply about Jesus' death and resurrection; it's about his kingdom as well. Yes, Jesus is the one who came and died for the sins of the world, taking it all to the cross, but in dying and rising back to life from the dead, he disarmed all the powers and forces of evil and then inaugurated his new reign—his kingdom—on earth. To Jesus, the kingdom *is* the gospel, and yes, he made it possible, but as we keep pointing to Jesus, he keeps pointing to the kingdom.

Why is this so important? Because it affects our whole mindset of what it means to be missional. If we send our kids out into the world to tell people about Jesus, we feel pretty good that we've done our job, even if it goes badly for them. But when Jesus sent out the seventy-two in Luke 10, they were simply told to demonstrate and tell others about the *kingdom*: "Heal the sick who are there and tell them, 'The kingdom of God has come near to you'" (verse 9). The message was the same when he sent out the Twelve: "As you go, proclaim this message: 'The kingdom of heaven has come near.' Heal the sick, raise the dead, cleanse those who have leprosy, drive out demons. Freely you have received; freely give" (Matthew 10:8).

We're not responsible for whether people respond to God's kingdom—Jesus made that pretty clear when he sent out the seventy-two—but living as kingdom people who seek to bring God's transformation into the lives of those around us means that others will experience what it looks like to be part of his kingdom. Just like my time with Fiona and her friends in the bar, showing what God's kingdom actually looks and feels like is much more effective than simply teaching a concept. If lives are to be truly transformed, the lived-experience of God's kingdom must come with an understanding about the King who reigns over it. But the explanation of the kingdom often comes after the demonstration.

So, Jesus doesn't want us settling for rhetoric about him. He wants us to demonstrate his works and ways as well as share his words. He wants his followers to look more like him, and he wants those who are gripped by the evil kingdom of this world to find hope and practical help. That's why he spent so much time on a hillside explaining the types of people and their unique characteristics that would get this beautiful work done in the world. The Sermon on the Mount was his great apprenticeship talk,[2] and we would be well served by making it the daily reading and daily pattern of our family life so that someday we will live out the words we read in Scripture.

Herein lies the gut check that every parent must settle before the mission begins: *Do we want Metroville Christianity or real kingdom Christianity to be the story we call our children into? Do we want normal kids, or do we want kids who march to a different drum? Do we want kids who can stand against the currents of normal life and who can innovate and create all that's new and good in their world? Do we want upside-down kids?*

LIVING OUT THE UPSIDE-DOWN KINGDOM

What does living this upside-down kingdom life really mean? And *why* are we living it? Well, if we want to see a world that looks like heaven, then we need to start living as Jesus called us to live. And what did he call us to do? Well, he called us to make disciples (Matthew 28:19–20), but he also called us to "seek first his kingdom" (Matthew 6:33), and that means being part of ushering in a world that looks like heaven on earth. It means no longer living a Metroville life that's all about meeting our individual, nuclear family needs, and instead looking to reach out, welcome, and meet the needs of the broken world around us, just as Jesus spent his time on earth doing.

And what's more, as families, we are called to live this way *together.*

If we're going to live the mission of God as a *family* story, it's going to require bravery and courage. At times it will mean shaking up our rhythms and routines a little, which might feel uncomfortable to begin with. Right now, we live in what theologians often call "the now and not yet" of God's kingdom, which basically means that, from God's perspective, the kingdom is here, but it's not yet here in its fullness. For now, we "see things imperfectly" (1 Corinthians 13:12 NLT), and the battle is still raging. We haven't got it all sewn up and sorted. We don't know what battles might lie ahead, what sacrifices we might have to make, what the personal costs might be for us as a family. And so living this kingdom life can feel risky. It means we have to fly blind and walk by faith, committing and investing our sacrifices and efforts in the hope that, in due time, we'll be really glad we did.

Taking our families on this adventure is the greatest opportunity to forge a life of following Jesus in our kids. It is only when we step out of what is known and familiar that we truly learn and grow. That's part of the *why* of living this life, too. It's only when we don't have all the answers and our comforts aren't all taken care of that we have to trust in God. It's in that risky faith-gap that we (and our kids) will learn to walk out what it means to be disciples of Jesus. That's why Jesus said, "You're blessed when you're at the end of your rope. With less of you there is more of God and his rule" (Matthew 5:3 MSG). When we make our lives less about us, we make more space for God.

When we choose to step out in faith together as a family,

it draws everyone closer together. The bonds that are formed as we run after a common kingdom purpose are stronger than when we try to fulfill our own needs. Those in our righteous brood share the same heart and passion as we run after the same things. When together you decide to welcome people in need into your home, or to address loneliness in your neighborhood, or to befriend a family in crisis, you not only learn to follow Jesus, but you also learn how to be a closer family. If you've ever been on a short-term missions trip, a team-building day, white-water rafting, or been part of an athletic team or military regiment, you know what this feels like—we get caught up in pursuing something beyond ourselves and relationships develop. As we choose to engage in God's mission together as families, our kids learn what it means to trust in Jesus for themselves; we become less obsessed about our own comforts and more focused on the needs of others; and we create greater depths of relationship as a family and with our wider community. We just need to take those first steps and trust that Jesus is bigger than our fears.

THE JESUS LIFE IS A LIFE OF RISK AND ADVENTURE OR IT'S NOT A LIFE AT ALL

Jesus drew his disciples into this adventurous and courageous life—and they took huge risks to follow him. "We have left all we had to follow you!" Peter tells Jesus (Luke 18:28). They ended up on a journey where they learned a lot, saw some amazing things happen, grew in relationship with one another, and ultimately became part of the greatest movement the world has ever seen. They gave up their lives for this story and this man, Jesus. Imagine the pride and humility and thankfulness they must have felt when they saw Jesus and their comrades when they passed over. To be able to say, "Yeah, we took a different path," or, "Wow, that cost us everything, but it was so worth it." Wouldn't those be the greatest experiences we could ever envision? Of course! But to get there, we've got to live differently than how other families live.

For the first two years after Ryan moved to the assisted living ranch, we took a breather. Sure, we still lived into God's mission, but I resigned from leading our church, and Cheryl and I obeyed the wisdom of our spiritual formation guides in taking a rest. We bought property in Denver and pursued Cheryl's lifelong dream of having a horse ranch, chickens, and more time together. As we enjoyed this two-year commercial break, we also regularly visited Ryan in Alton.

Each time we'd fly into St. Louis to see Ryan, we'd head over the mighty Mississippi to this alluring, albeit struggling, river town. And each time we did, we wondered why such a beautiful town was so busted up. Alton had lost over 60 percent of its population since the 1960s, half the homes were "slumlord" owned, and the yearly average family income was $22,000. Almost half the population was African American, yet you could count the African American business owners on one hand, especially in the downtown area. Beautiful buildings were boarded up and homes were in disarray, but the spirit of the town seemed to call out for a little encouragement.

On one particular trip, Cheryl and I were talking to a waitress at an Italian restaurant, who shared about the drug use among young people in Alton. As we left, Cheryl stopped walking the sidewalk, and as I turned around to see why she was lagging behind, she said, "Why don't we sell the ranch, move here, and see if we can do something to help out around this town?"

As we stood on the sidewalk, staring at each other, I made it pretty obvious that I was not ready to leave our new life of peace. I really had no interest in starting another mission, especially if it meant leaving the beautiful surroundings and the community we had formed in Denver to move to the Midwest. No offense intended, but I just wasn't feeling it, if you know what I mean. To get her in the car and to kick the can down the road, I said, "Babe, let's head back home, and if it still feels like we should move here, we can pray about it and maybe pray about it some more and then maybe talk about it some more. And then maybe we'll pray for another year or two."

She knew I wasn't interested. That's what Christians often do to *not* go on mission. We talk and pray about things, but we don't go.

So, with that we went home, and Cheryl started pestering me.

"So can we talk about Alton?" she asked on morning number one. "Have you been praying about it?"

On day two, three, four, and five she asked the same thing.

"Yeah, of course I've been praying about it," I lied.

"But what is Jesus saying to you?" she asked.

"Well, I think he's saying we should stay here and rest a bit," I replied.

"Wow!" she quipped. "It's like we have two Jesuses in our home, because I'm pretty dang sure my Jesus is telling us to go!"

The fight continued for a few weeks. To quell the ruckus, I called for a family meeting. My two daughters—one newly married and one newly engaged—were home with their partners, and so I thought I could count on them to help Cheryl come to her senses.

I seem to remember starting the family talk by saying something like, "Cheryl, tell them your stupid idea to leave paradise for purgatory ... ."

As she shared her heart for Alton, it was like watching the Grinch's frown turn upside down all over my family. One by one they all stated not only that they thought we should go, but that they wanted to go with us!

That day, as everyone sided with Cheryl, I remember being both upset that it meant moving away from the life we'd built in Denver, but also amazed, inspired, and proud that, as adults, our kids still wanted to be with us and be on mission with us. As I write this, I'm tearing up again thinking about the privilege it has been to have them with us now for over five years in Alton.

Alli and Matthew have taken to a life of foster care. Matthew is an Alton firefighter. McKenna started Commons Yoga and was employed by a local social agency working with difficult abuse cases. Now she is a counselor at one of the high schools in Ferguson, Missouri, just fifteen minutes away. Her husband, Jessie, is a math teacher and football coach at Alton High School and is an inspiration and leader simply by being the only male African American teacher in a school with 45 percent Black students.

Together, we all started Lantern Network and Post Commons, which is an incubator for good works in Alton. We have an all-day-brunch café, a coffee roasting company, yoga studio, artist studio, coworking space, and an events space—and we try to help others start neighborhood missional communities and anything else that helps and encourages our city. Post Commons was a disused building that we renovated, and it has become the "living room" for our town. Every day we thank God for giving us unique pathways into the people and struggling plight of Alton. This entire mess is what the forty or so folks that are building this ecosystem with us call "church."

Every adventure we've gone on with God has required us to push into the unknown. But every time we've done that, we've formed a bond with each other and our community that not only deepens our walk with God but also shapes the world around us with the incoming of the kingdom.

As followers of Jesus, we can become part of someone and

something much bigger than ourselves, but to do that will mean counteracting the Metroville way of life.

Let me unpack a little more of what this has looked like in our community in Alton, as we've sought to counter the three giants we talked about in the previous chapter: individualism, consumerism, and materialism.

Countering Individualism with Community

We are currently part of a community that includes about twenty families who are all committed to a common mission centered around Post Commons. Some of the families moved into town with us because they wanted to be part of what we are doing, and some we met along the way. As I mentioned earlier, the population of Alton has dramatically decreased in the last fifty years, so there are a lot of deserted spaces and there are very few ministries to help kids at all. This town of thirty thousand people has no visible youth center, youth ministry, or outlets for kids. Just twenty minutes away is a suburb with beautiful recreation centers, sports clubs, and parks—it's the kind of area families from all over flock to because of what it delivers for the "personal development" of their children.

Yet, I see some things happening in our people that I often don't see in over-resourced communities. Our children play together at local parks, and they learn to meet and relate to kids and parents of different walks of life, skin color, and economic level. They watch their parents do the same, and as they are growing up, I'm seeing them developing a community identity instead of a personal identity.

One of the homes in our community takes in two homeless men, another home cares for a neighborhood single mom, and yet another family fosters several children. All the families in our community rally round these situations. They are watching and participating firsthand in a communal story that will forever frame their faith and sense of mission.

We have a GroupMe app that everyone in our extended spiritual family shares. Almost daily there are devotional thoughts, prayer requests, needs, and thanks communicated. This tears down the natural individualism that is crippling the church, and it is one of the most amazing things to be part of.

Our kids learn that they don't have just one or two brothers or sisters; they have twenty-three brothers and sisters and six to eight moms and dads that they feel comfortable with. As they grow, they'll know they can call anyone in the community for help along the way. Imagine if your kids grew up with memories of adults, teens, and friends who all moved in a tangible rhythm of life together. I'm guessing it will be a story they'll want to repeat.

Countering Consumerism with Contribution

In our church—our "extended spiritual family"—we fight consumerism by asking people to "own" the mission, whatever that mission may be. The antithesis to the consumer identity is the "producer" identity. Rather than shaping our lives around what we can get, we look at how we can contribute, what we can create, what we can take responsibility for, what solutions we can offer. This puts the focus outside of ourselves, and helps our kids grow up looking to contribute and serve rather than feeling entitled.

If the street we live on has an ugly fence that's been lying on the sidewalk for years, we don't complain about it; we put the fence back up. If kids are being bullied at the bus stop, we don't drive our kids to school; we walk out to the bus stop with them until the atmosphere changes. If our schools lack resources, we get the teachers what they need to serve the kids. When there isn't a coffee shop to hang out and meet people in, we don't move to the richer suburb with six coffee shops; we make one for our own town. When our city struggles with fatherless homes, delinquency, crime and all the normal "crappy town" stats, we foster kids, we coach football at the high school, we start nonprofits to work with the chronically poor and underserved, we teach in the harder schools, we buy homes in the tougher areas. *We own it!*

It's God's world, broken and bruised, and as his family, we are the only ones he has who will willingly dive in with him. And even the kids can get involved and contribute, whatever their age. The teenagers might help at the soup kitchen, and the toddlers might visit the retirement village to do art with seniors. We might get everyone working on a local park clean-up. The artistic types might create some street art to bring beauty to a local neighborhood. Whatever the activity, what we're learning is that several families, committed to owning a community instead of consuming it, can literally change a town ... or at the very least it will change those families.

Countering Materialism with Sharing

In our community we fight materialism by sharing all of our stuff. Seriously, sometimes we run a muffin pan across town so someone doesn't have to go to Target to buy one! We share cars, extra rooms in homes, campers, vacation rentals, or airline miles to help people vacation without all the costs. When we have big events at our events center, we send out a request for help, and a handful show up for an hour or two without expecting to be paid. When our young couples buy their first homes, us old guys offer to help with remodeling projects and give our time away. And it's all so beautiful to see and experience. Cheryl and I annually try to find ways to lower our monthly financial needs so that we can live more freely and give more away.

Our entire community has experienced what downsizing and descending does for our spirit—and we love it! Do our kids lack stuff? Do we have to delay some things? Do we sometimes have to say no to big purchases or overindulgence? *Yes.* But what we gain is of much greater worth.

So, do you all need to move to Alton and join in with the Post Commons so that your family can live on mission? Well, we'd love to have you, but I'm pretty sure God's got a plan to see his kingdom come in every part of the world. If you live in that nicer suburb with the recreation centers and coffee shops, does living this upside-down kingdom mean you have to move? That might be what God's calling you to do. But it might be that he's calling you to stay right where you are and to intentionally look out for the needs all around you—because, believe me, there will still be a hunger and need for real community in that place. The needs might not seem as obvious, but there will be loneliness, marriage breakdowns, crippling debt, and insecurity in parenting.

Seeking the kingdom, wherever you are, will always involve some challenge and some inconvenience. Your family won't be able to live that Metroville life if you want to really follow Jesus. In order to see the needs around you, you'll need to slow down a bit and find space in your family life to connect more meaningfully with others in your neighborhood so that your free time isn't just for yourselves but embeds you in the community around you. You'll need to push into the spaces where things aren't always certain; where your time, your money, and your resources aren't always your own. All this can sound difficult, but the prize is more than worth the cost. You'll have a front-row seat in seeing God move in people's lives. You'll create friendships with others on the journey— bonds that are way more significant than the fellowship of Bible study groups. And your kids will grow in a faith that is active and real—an adventure in the kingdom of heaven that is far more likely to help them know how to follow Jesus and live for him throughout their lives.

IN SUMMARY

- Our family needs to know the good news of God's kingdom before we go on mission together, so that we know *why* we're doing it.

- Good news is about the transformation of real life for real people, not just about living a good life and getting into heaven when we die.

- Jesus said we don't have to wait for God's kingdom—it's at hand now—so we can pray for all of his kingdom to be evident in our own lives and in the lives of those around us.

- This is a risky and adventurous way to live, but Jesus calls us to live this upside-down kingdom life *together*. When we seek a mission beyond ourselves, together, bonds of relationship are formed.

- Living like this means countering individualism with community, consumerism with contribution, and materialism with sharing.

SOMETHING TO THINK ABOUT

- In what ways does your view of Christianity reflect more of "Churchianity" than seeing God's kingdom come on earth?

- What are the barriers stopping you from living a kingdom life?

- Who are you on this journey with? Are there other friends and families you can live a kingdom adventure with?

- How could you live as a family to counteract individualism, consumerism, and materialism with community, contribution, and sharing?

MAKE IT HAPPEN

- Think about what the "good news" of Jesus could look like to the people around you. How could you share that good news in both word and deed?

- Make a list of friends, individuals, or families who might be up for this adventure with you. Invite at least one person/family over for food this next week and chat with them about what you've read in this chapter.

- Pick one idea for counteracting individualism, consumerism, and materialism, and try it out as a family over the next month.

4

THE ALTAR: WHERE THE MISSIONAL FAMILY IS BORN

As a pastor, one of my great joys is to be able to officiate weddings. Every once in a while, however, the experience is destroyed by overbearing parents—a bit like Steve Martin in the 1991 movie *Father of the Bride*. Because the wedding day is built up to be so special, it's not unusual for people to get uptight, fight over a wedding dress, or micromanage how the cake gets decorated. But amidst the normal stress, I often see a sad scenario where the parents can't give the kids any space and try to take ownership over the entire ceremony ... and then their lives afterward.

I remember one particular instance when the poor bride-to-be came to see me before the rehearsal. "I just can't go through with this!" she told me through her sobs. I thought I was going to have to talk her into staying with her future husband, but the issue wasn't him. It was her overbearing parents who were trying to control her and her fiancé, all the preparations, and the wedding itself.

After she vented through many tears, I promised I would handle it. As the rehearsal was about to begin, I confronted the mother and father and told them I was running the show and that their only job was to shut up, smile, and agree with everything I was directing them to do. By my tone, I knew they understood how serious I was … but it didn't help. When the wedding day came, we were all stressed! All I could tell the poor couple was, "It will soon be over." Fortunately, God has a sense of humor, and we all got to enjoy watching the mother trip on the first stair leading up to lighting the unity candles. She stumbled and then managed to catch her Ace-Ventura haircut on fire as her head smacked into the candelabra. Everyone gasped as we batted down the flame.

The rest of the proceedings went off without incident, but I, as well as this couple, knew that they had a long miserable life ahead because of her parents' perceived "ownership" over them and inability to let go.

Whenever I do pre-marital counseling, I base it on findings about four issues that can kill a marriage: sex, money, disagreements, and leaving and cleaving.

The biblical idea of leaving and cleaving is laid out in Genesis 2:24: "Therefore shall a man *leave* his father and his mother, and shall *cleave* unto his wife: and they shall be one flesh" (KJV, emphases mine). It's built into God's design that husbands and wives are to be intimately linked, and this can only happen when parents learn they must someday truly "let go" so that the couple can become one. The reason I make sure to spend an entire week of preparation on this is because it's such a huge problem.

OWNERS VS. STEWARDS

Parents often feel like *owners*—that we created our kids; that we are solely responsible for their upbringing, protection, provision, and future. And when someone feels that they *own* something or someone, it makes them act crazy. They can miss the blessing of being able to prepare and send their children into the world. Whether it be a father who abusively yells at his kids from the bleachers, or a mother who withholds her blessing because her child doesn't get straight As in school, or the father who tries to vicariously live out his own dreams through his children—a sense of ownership may be one of the most debilitating misconceptions parents can have.

The Scriptures teach that we really don't own anything. Everything is given to us by God, and our role is simply that of being *stewards*.

Matthew 25—the Scripture often referred to as the parable of the talents—teaches us how God views humanity as we take care of what he gives us. The point of the parable is that we will be held accountable not for what we produce, but for what we do with what God gives to us. One of my favorite passages for parents is found in Psalm 127:3–5, and it says, "Children are a gift from the Lord; they are a reward from him. Children born to a young man are like arrows in a warrior's hands. How joyful is the man whose quiver is full of them!" (NLT).

What a cool metaphor. Our children are not ours. They are God's. He created them and entrusts them to us as if they were arrows in our quiver.

I'm not sure if you've heard, but the US has a national shortage of umpires for kids' sports programs. Why? Simply because parents have gotten so verbally and physically abusive during games that people are no longer willing to put themselves on the line for $15 an hour. Parents who feel they *own* their kids will often show it by lashing out and trying to control the situations in their children's lives; they will yell offensive, threatening words at a seventeen-year-old ump. Those with a *steward* mentality would see a game loss, or a missed foul call, or even a sidelining injury, as an opportunity to develop the child's character.

Parents who feel they *own* their kids might go into debt to pay for expensive fashion, tech, or extra-curricular activities— just to keep up with the Joneses or simply because they think it makes their kids happy. But *stewards* may ask their kids to work to pay for part of these costs, or even tell their kids, "We can't afford that this year." They might limit extra-curricular activities so that they have more time together as a family and to be involved in the mission God's called them to—trusting that God will provide all the experiences, talents, and skills their kids really need. *Owners* push harsh expectations on kids. *Stewards* challenge, but let their kids grow in due time. *Owners* micromanage their kids' schoolwork and put pressure on them to achieve. *Stewards* act more like coaches, equipping and training their kids to take responsibility for their academic work.

The key difference between being an owner and a steward, according to the parable of the talents, is that the owner is doing everything for themselves, whereas the steward is basing every decision, action, and word on pleasing the real owner. Thus, the steward is always asking the question, "How can I partner with God in growing his child into the man or woman he wants them to become?" This is why parenting in the upside-down kingdom of God looks different from parenting in Metroville. Ultimately, we're growing our kids in the things of God, not the things of the world.

I remember one time when my daughters and my wife were talking together about why I didn't yell and scream on the hockey bleachers like all the other dads. They thought it was because I didn't care. I used the opportunity to tell them that I cared most about who they were becoming and how I simply enjoyed watching them do anything: winning, losing, drinking water from the Gatorade dispenser, fixing their gloves, laughing with their friends, enjoying their team, listening to their coach. "I just love watching you both enjoy hockey and life," I told them. "So I don't get that amped about the win or loss. I'm just proud to be your dad." I think they liked my answer.

The reality is that, as stewards, we are responsible for some things, but we can't take responsibility for everything.

We *are* responsible for teaching our kids God's truths. We are responsible for modeling the unconditional love of the Father, and for doing our utmost to let our kids know that they are valuable, loveable creations of God. We are responsible for modeling the way of kingdom living. We are responsible for being real and asking for forgiveness when we screw up, and granting forgiveness when they screw up. We are responsible for working hard to provide as many life-giving opportunities as we can, while balancing rest, fun, hard work, school, and life in community. We are responsible for giving our kids access and options to choose a good path and find their way toward their calling.

We *are not* responsible for the choices they make, or the pain or triumph that happens along the way. We are not responsible for covering for their sins, or making their way easy, or shielding them from reality. We are not responsible for who they become.

In the end, moms and dads who take seriously the life of the steward sleep a little better, knowing that God will do the heavy lifting and will give his favor to parents who work with him on growing great people.

SLAYING THE IDOL OF FAMILY

If you ask parents to define their job, most would say something that includes the words "provide for" and "protect from." For sure, as our kids are developing, we must do both of these, or our kids will starve or fall out of trees. So yes, we must provide for and protect from, but neither of these should remain the focus for the duration of our parenting season. As Christians, the main objective of parenting is to create, develop, and inspire our kids to be authentic lovers of Jesus and his mission and to be willing to suffer and maybe even die for his sake.

I realize no parent wants to hear this, but if we are to step into God's mission together, we have to acknowledge the reality that our family must not become an idol. We cannot be so fearful for our kids' safety that we fail to entrust them into God's hands and fully participate in his mission. We cannot use our kids as an excuse to be too busy, too stressed, or too broke to take part in God's work in the world. Sometimes you will need to model what it means to sacrifice for Jesus. They might need to hear Mom say, "Kids, I know we're all tired, and we all just really want to watch TV, but this evening the Browns really need our help. Mrs. Brown had a bad fall, and we've offered to clean up their house together. Let's ask God to give us energy, grace, and patience so that we can put aside our own wants and needs and go and help the Browns."

Or they might need to hear Daddy say, "Joey, I know you're sad that Daddy can't tuck you in tonight, but sometimes Daddy needs to help other people, and tonight is one of those nights. Please pray for Daddy and ask God to give you peace with sharing Daddy."

God is always extending and building family. I touched on this in chapter two, but remember when Jesus' mother was trying to get his attention, and his buddies tried to get him to come away from the party to go to his mother? Jesus said, "Who is my mother, and who are my brothers?" (Matthew 12:48). Everyone around him must have leaned in to find out the answer to the riddle: "Whoever does the will of my Father in heaven" (verse 50). In a culture where your family had to be first place, he was teaching people that the biological family was now second place to the family he was building.

If it were up to me, I'd probably not call you to this level of challenge. I'm a people pleaser, so I prefer you just be happy. But now that I'm about thirty years into our story, I'm more certain than ever of the need to call you to God's bigger family—and away from risk management, safe environments, and small visions for your kids. The gospel of Jesus is the wildest, most life-reorienting vortex you can ever be drawn into, and I think your greatest joy will be to reveal that to your kids and help them live into it.

And someday, it will feel pretty cool to stand with your kids before Jesus and see him give everyone a wink, a big thumbs up, and to hear him say, "Thanks! It was a blast to watch your family live such a large life!"

YOU CAN'T HAVE A MISSION WITHOUT AN ALTAR

As I mentioned earlier, Abraham's was the first missional family. God asked Abraham to leave his country and his people and head out by himself on an unknown mission that would eventually lead to his forming a new tribe. But, as often happens, some time elapses between the big call of God and the fruition of God's promise (that he would make Abraham into "a great nation"[1]). Abraham and his wife, Sarah, wait and wait and wait. Then finally, even though they are now old in age, God miraculously helps them conceive a son they name Isaac.

In a strange twist, God calls Abraham to sacrifice that son. Maybe you can imagine yourself processing this request. Just do the math. *If God takes my son, how can I make a "great nation"? I'll have no lineage. God's great plan and mission will go nowhere.*

But Abraham clearly wasn't doing the math that morning. He held out hope against what he saw and heard, and trusted God to somehow pull a rabbit out of the hat.

He loaded up a small party of family and friends and headed out for a three-day journey to the mountain to sacrifice his son. Each night they would have had time around the fire pit, lying next to each other, looking at the stars. And then, after Isaac would fall asleep, Abraham—tense and severely confused—would walk, stare up into the black unknown, and weep, wonder, and wish God's mission wasn't so costly.

Most of you know how the story goes. Once on the mountain, Abraham makes an altar, binds his son on bundles of kindling that Isaac helped him gather, and then readies a knife to plunge into the heart of all his hopes and dreams … his boy.

At the last second, God saves the day, asks Abraham to put the knife down, and Abraham learns the most important lesson in having a missional family: The first thing we have to do is give our kids back to God.[2]

There's not a parent alive who doesn't shudder at the thought of this. But God's interaction with Abraham demonstrates that trusting him with our children is an act of faith: faith in his unfailing love and in his eternal perspective.

For most of us in a Western context, Christianity (or *Churchianity*) is like chicken soup for the soul. We read our Bible, attend church, listen to sermons, and try to get our children through all the age-appropriate ministries in hopes that they will adopt our moral compass, be good people, and succeed in life. For sure, nothing is wrong with these hopes and dreams for our kids.

But to follow Jesus is first and foremost a death story. It is not an upwardly mobile, gated-community, country-club story. We are a downwardly mobile, countercultural people who are called to swim against the currents of consumerism, individualism, and materialism. Under Jesus' brand of life, we give up things, delay gratification, and sell our possessions if it might help someone. We risk, and we serve, and we deny our flesh, so that God's kingdom will come here and now.

In Philippians 2 we see that God became a man, and then as a man took the form of a slave and went to the cross: "he made himself nothing by taking the very nature of a servant, being made in human likeness. And being found in appearance as a man, he humbled himself by becoming obedient to death—even death on a cross!" (verses 7–8).

In ancient spiritual formation, we say Jesus taught us the "cruciform" way (the way of the cross). God-Man-Servant-Death. It is downward all the way—but then God exalts and lifts him back up. We are told to have this same attitude, this same trajectory, and to trust that, in due time, everything we sacrificed and risked and lost will produce *shalom*,* beauty, and lasting fruit.

Moms, dads—if your goal for your children doesn't include preparing, teaching, and modeling the way of the cross, the cruciform way, even unto death, then I'm not sure we really believe the story.

When my youngest, McKenna, stood in between her best friend and her abusive boyfriend who was trying to attack her, McKenna took the brunt of his violence. The concussion she

---

* *Shalom*—defined as "peace, wholeness, completeness and well-being—is rooted in Scripture and in the nature of God." See Cath Livesey, *Holy Disruption: Harnessing the Prophetic to Shape a More Christlike Church* (Wyoming: 100 Movements Publishing, 2022), 8.

experienced brought an end to her D1 hockey scholarship—and all the investment we had made for eight years.

When our daughter, Alli, and her husband, Matthew, chose to live in a very rough area of Alton where young men were being gunned down a hundred feet from their house, we had to trust and let God lead their lives.

One of the best things we can do for our kids is to teach them not to fear dying. One day when McKenna was struggling with anxiety over some school tests, I asked her what she was really afraid of. I kept saying, "So what's the very worst thing that can happen if you get a B, or a C, or flunk the entire class?"

We kept going down the rabbit trail and eventually made it to the end. I told her, "So no matter what, the worst thing that can happen isn't that bad. You're not going to die from this test. And even if, for some odd reason, the stress did kill you, you'd get to live in a place without any more tests! There's nothing to fear at all—even dying. And if you don't fear death, then you surely don't have to fear living."

Now you might be thinking that conversation seems a bit extreme, especially over a school test! But the reality is that the way we approach these everyday situations with our kids often says a lot about our whole life perspective and vision for them. And so, parents, consider your motives. Are you seeking to develop a brood of stout-hearted missionaries? If your answer is yes, then you picked the right answer! Anything less will actually leave our kids more vulnerable.

Let them try and fail.

Let them risk.

Let them give their money and time to people who need it.

Let them become close friends with those in poverty, those on the other side of the tracks, those who don't share their sexuality or world views or behavioral morals.

We must give our kids this freedom because the real world is full of harsh realities and people who aren't like us. There's no way to avoid it. And to be honest, it's better for them to face these things while they are at home, where we can have discussions in a safe environment and often the consequences are less serious. At some point you've got to help your kids grow and show them that there's nothing to be afraid of—except being out of step with God.

God owns us, our kids, and our calling. Growing a family that will serve God to the fullest begins with us putting our children back on the altar and trusting God with their future. To steward their precious lives means we must let go!

Owners try to grow their kids in their own likeness.

Godly stewards grow their kids in the likeness of Jesus.

And for our kids to cleave to Jesus, we must get them ready to leave us by apprenticing them in his ways.

IN SUMMARY

- Parents often feel like "owners," but we're actually "stewards" of our kids.

- When we're stewards, we focus on raising our kids in a way that pleases God (who is the real owner) and trust him to lead our kids' lives.

- We need to know what we are and aren't responsible for. We *are* responsible for teaching our kids God's truths, modeling unconditional love, and letting them know they are valuable creations of God. We *are* responsible for providing opportunities/access to paths that lead toward fulfillment of their calling. And we *are* responsible for modeling kingdom living, asking forgiveness, and granting forgiveness. We are *not* responsible for the choices they make, the pain or triumph they experience, covering up for their sins, making life easy, or shielding them from reality. We are not responsible for who they become.

- When we teach our kids not to fear anything (including dying), they are free to live this missional life.

SOMETHING TO THINK ABOUT

- Do you parent as an "owner" or a "steward"?

- Are there any specific ways that the "owner" attitude manifests in the way you parent your kids?

- How might you address that attitude and become a steward of your kids in those particular areas?

- Where are you doing well at taking responsibility for your kids in the things that God calls you to?

- In what ways might you model sacrificial living to your kids?

MAKE IT HAPPEN

- If there is an area where you act more like an "owner" with your kids, consider a different approach you could take. Pray about it, share with your spouse or a friend, and put it into action.

- Where/when could you say "yes" to something (age appropriate), to give your kids more freedom, while choosing to trust that God is leading their lives?

- What could you do to show your kids how Jesus calls us to a sacrificial life? It could be serving another family, helping out a friend at a cost to your own family resources, volunteering, or raising money for a cause as a family. Invite your kids to join you in this.

5

RAISING KINGDOMLINGS

As a professional house painter, if I wanted to teach someone the trade, I wouldn't just hire a young man, pay him a small wage, and ask him to observe me painting for a summer. Sure, if he casually watched me from his seated position on the back of my tailgate for three or four months, he could probably explain some correct concepts about house painting to a friend. But if I wanted to make a real painter of this young man, I'd have to call him off the tailgate, give him absolutely every tool I had, and help him learn firsthand every aspect of painting. He'd have to get dirty, deal with his fears, take responsibility, and so on.

It's the same when we're discipling our kids. "Discipleship" is a word most Christian parents know, and we generally understand it to mean teaching our children (or a convert) the truths of Scripture, the doctrine and theology of God, and establishing the moral codes of the faith. All this is good—but only if we understand the fuller meaning of Jesus' idea of what a disciple is. When he used the word, he actually meant what we might call an "apprentice." The word for "disciple" comes from the Latin *discipulus*, which means "pupil or learner." And it seems pretty clear that, to Jesus, to learn meant to both hear and obey. That's why Jesus rounded off the Sermon on the Mount with a call to put his words into practice: "Therefore everyone who hears these words of mine and puts them into practice is like a wise man who built his house on the rock" (Matthew 7:24). Apprenticeship involves putting into practice the things we have learned.

LIVING THE LIFE OF GOD

God wants us to form more than doctrine, theology, and moral codes in our kids. He wants us to form the very life of Jesus in them.[1] True discipleship isn't achieved until the person has learned to live the life of God. That's what it means to apprentice someone in the ways of Jesus.

Discipling a child as an apprentice puts the onus on the parents. Not the senior pastor. Not the kids pastor. Not the youth pastor. Not on any other staff member at your church. Yes, pastoral staff can disciple your kids, but the one who is designed to spend the most time, and who can actually model the life of Jesus, is you! Our kids will learn more about what it means to love Jesus and participate in his work by watching you than anyone else in their life. That's a big call, and we can only do it in Christ's strength, empowered by his Spirit.

In 2 Corinthians 3:1–3, Paul talks about us being like "living letters"—people who demonstrate how we are to follow Jesus. If someone spent a week with you, fully able to see how you use your time and your resources, what would they say you value? That's not meant to induce a guilt trip, but it is worth consciously asking ourselves what our values are, and how we live those out in such a way that our lives become living letters to our kids—lives that tell the story of Jesus in our words and actions.

A misunderstanding of discipleship tends to create Pharisees, but true discipleship creates kingdom citizens—or what I like to call *kingdomlings*. It's a strange concept, but Jesus actually warned his apprentices to watch out for the "yeast of the Pharisees" (Matthew 16:6). The yeast (or "leaven") was the law/doctrine-focused spiritual fervency that prevented the Pharisees from truly loving people. Jesus didn't come to belittle the Pharisees or to suggest that scriptural knowledge and moral living was bad, but he did come to fulfill, enlarge, and expand what true spiritual formation was.[2] He came to model a holistic life where doctrine, theology, knowledge, and morality were coupled with love, mercy, faith, and action.

Although Western non-participatory discipleship tends to shrivel our kids' hearts, active discipleship (apprenticeship) helps Jesus come alive in them, and that's what causes them to love their King. Imagine being taught all the theory of how to play a musical instrument but never being given the opportunity to actually touch it. If you've ever known the enjoyment of playing a piece of beautiful music, you'll know that the theory just doesn't cut it. You actually have to play to get the full enjoyment from your learning. Not only that, but you have to keep playing, keep putting what you learn into practice; otherwise, you quickly lose your ability to use the skills you're learning. It's the same with discipling our kids. If it's all theory in their heads, they don't ever truly learn to enjoy and love God, and they never experience the "fullness of life"[3] Jesus came to bring us.

Paul summed up the power of kingdom discipleship this way (and it should be the goal of every parent): "until Christ is *formed* in you" (Galatians 4:19, emphasis mine). As parents, we are to help form Christ in our kids ... the *whole* life of Jesus, not just the words about Jesus. True spiritual formation therefore cannot happen through sermons or Bible studies. It includes those things, but it mostly happens as we let our humanity become like the humanity of Jesus—and as we help our kids to do the same.

HOLISTICALLY FORMING CHRIST IN OUR KIDS' LIVES

Helping form Christ in our kids is one of the greatest privileges of being a parent. But what does that actually look like? Well, it strikes me there are three areas we can focus on:

- The **Head** (mind) of Jesus: *having the same focus as Christ and viewing the world as he does.*

- The **Heart** of Jesus: *allowing our hearts to break over the things that break Jesus' heart.*
- The **Hands** (mission) of Jesus: *embodying the good news of Jesus and doing the work of God on earth.*

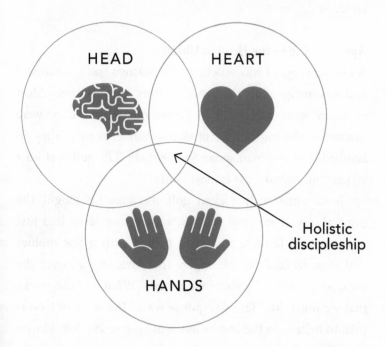

Most of us want our kids to develop the heart or head of Jesus, but we're a bit less certain about the hands of Jesus. The heart seems pretty safe, but honestly, if your children get the heart of Jesus, they may choose to live a life of service that makes you squirm. If they have the head (mind) of Jesus, they may not pursue the American Dream as many of us have. They may instead seek justice, live for the poor, put themselves in harm's way—all because they love Jesus.

So, the gut check begins with us.

Do you really want *all* of Jesus to be formed in your children?

Apprenticing in the Head of Christ

A few years ago, I was watching The Masters golf tournament and was intrigued by the commentators' conversations. Most of them were successful ex-professionals, and they were discussing the importance of skill versus mentality. They all laughed, and one man spoke for them all: "Oh, golf is at least 90 percent mental ... as is most of life."

Jesus apparently played golf, because he taught the same thing. If we read John 6, we see that Jesus had just miraculously fed five thousand people with a few nibbles and then walked on the water. The buzz was all over the area, and eventually someone asked, "What are the works that we must do?" Jesus' response was, "The work of God is this: to believe in the one he has sent" (verse 29). Jesus knew something that we are sometimes slow to understand: Faith, good deeds, wisdom, purity, right living, and supernatural power all depend upon whether or not someone actually believes.

A great definition of a disciple is someone who moves from unbelief to belief in every aspect of their life. Think about that. When a Christian gets a diagnosis of cancer, for example, they might believe God for eternal life beyond the grave—and face death with courage and peace—but they might not have ever trusted Jesus with their finances. Or another person might have learned to believe that God will provide for their needs but struggles to believe God in the area of their personal calling. In a real sense, we are all partial believers. We believe some of what Jesus teaches, and yet we struggle to believe him in other areas. Like the father of the demon-possessed son, all of us, to some extent, say, "I do believe; help me overcome my unbelief!" (Mark 9:24). So, discipling our kids isn't about just trying to get them to believe in Jesus. The hardest work is getting them to believe what Jesus believes.

As a starting point, you need to know what *you* actually believe.

Take a minute to consider what your family manifesto would include. A manifesto is like a set of core beliefs that, if you were on your deathbed, you'd want to impart as wisdom to guide your children through their lives. For me, a manifesto is like a tattoo—and I actually have a few tattoos that are a living picture of what is important for me in how I live my life. Deuteronomy 11 talks about telling our children the stories of what God has done and writing those things on our doorposts as a reminder. If we want to believe what Jesus believed, and to apprentice our kids in that too, we need to really take hold of what those core things are. It's easy to get caught up in the side details of what the Christian life is about, or to think that our kids will pick up their core beliefs from the lessons they receive from church—but you are the most influential person in your child's life, which means you have an amazing opportunity to instill those core values and to show them a living picture of following Jesus.

Rather than relying on Sunday school lessons, when we know our core beliefs and live them out, we can point back to what God is doing in our lives and help our kids understand those core beliefs for themselves. (This is where the head, heart, and hands often intersect.)

What might apprenticing in the head of Jesus look like in practice? Well, if one of our kids is afraid, we show them love and remind them of their identity in Jesus—because our core belief is that love overcomes fear.

Or if one of our kids is being vengeful toward a sibling, we talk about forgiveness, grace, and kindness—because our core belief is that God shows us mercy and requires the same of us.

Or if we're encouraging our kids to be generous and grateful for what they have, we can talk about our core belief that God's heart is for the poor.

Or if we mess up as parents (because we all do!), we say we are sorry and ask for forgiveness, including from our kids—because our core belief is that we have all fallen short and need to repent and receive forgiveness.

I'd encourage you to write down a few of your core values, maybe even on a board that you hang in your house for everyone to see, or in a family journal, which also contains favorite Scriptures, sayings, memories, and specific words for each of your kids related to their identity, their mission, and how you pray over them. As your kids grow, it could be a place where they add their own defining Scriptures and values that mean a lot to them.

In order to apprentice our kids in the head of Christ, we need to know the core beliefs we want to instill in our kids. But how do we actually make that a reality, so that they increasingly have the mind of Jesus? Here are four key areas that will help you put this into practice.

Feed the brain. Cheryl and I regularly read Scripture to our kids. Granted, a child's brain isn't developed fully, and it takes about twenty-one years for cause-and-effect to actually take hold in the young brain, but I figure it's always good to get the words of Jesus into the mind early. There's a story of a man passing another man and his two dogs heading up a mountain pass. The man descending asked, "Which one of those dogs gets to the top first?" The dog owner replied, "Whichever one I feed the most."

Whether it's reading Scripture, memorizing Scripture, or talking through the teachings of Jesus, I think it's just good to feed the brain. For sure, the world will put other food in our kids' brains, so I at least want to feed them God's thoughts even if they can't recall them or figure out what they mean. Even now, with our girls aged twenty-five and twenty-six, Cheryl still sends out devotional thoughts to everyone in our family.

Give them a window into what you believe. Our kids will learn a lot from just watching us, but sometimes it's helpful for us to verbalize why we do what we do, so we help our kids join the dots of what it means to follow Jesus and put that into practice. For example, our kids might see us making cakes for a bake sale for refugees. That's good in itself, but sometimes it's also good to explain how that connects with God's heart. We might say to our kids something like, "Dad's making cakes for the bake sale because he cares about helping people in crisis, and that's because God cares about those people, too."

Cheryl and I love spending time with our grandkids. The other night, Mila (age four) was with "Papa" (that's me) in the top of the barn getting some hay for the horses. She loves to be in the barn, hanging out, and we talk about everything. Usually there's a life lesson, maybe even a saying I pass on to her that I got from my parents, but somewhere in our quality time, I usually drop a teaching or a thought I want her to remember.

"Hey, Mila, Papa will always love you, and I couldn't love anyone more than I love you, but you know who loves you even more than Papa?"

"Gigi?" she replies.

"Nope," I say. "Jesus … he made all of us, and he loves us more than we can ever love each other. So always remember, if you ever feel like you need a hug but no one's around, that Jesus is with you everywhere you go, and although you can't see him, he's there and is always looking at you and smiling."

Help them to engage with God in ways that relate to who they are. The Scriptures warn against embittering our kids,[4] which I think happens when we force them to go to or do religious things when their hearts aren't into it. If you've got practically minded kids, then doing a family devotion around the dinner table might not cut it. They might learn more by watching you do stuff and then explaining why you're doing what you're doing—as I mentioned above. Our kids grew up experiencing church as fun meetings in our home, parties, baptisms at the park, and pig roasts—all with our neighborhood relational networks and their own friends—so church was integrated in everything we did. Our kids seemed to love every part of it.

As they grew into their high school years, McKenna liked to have me lie next to her at night and pray with her. Alli would just text me, "I'm ready"—which meant she wanted me to come down and give her a fist bump, but she didn't seem to want me to do any prayer or Bible study with her. I was fine with that because I knew she had her Bible under her pillow—and letting her grow her own relationship with Jesus was much more significant than me controlling what she was learning from the Bible or making sure she said her prayers every night.

The most important thing is that they are fed and encouraged to own their faith. If we tangibly live out our own faith, our kids will probably desire it for themselves. If we have one foot in and one foot out, they'll probably bolt when given the opportunity.

Teach them to be curious. Encourage your kids to question everything, and think about great questions you can ask them.

When Alli was in eighth grade, she told me she was done being a Christian. Instead of freaking out, I simply asked, "Why?" And then she shared how the Christian kids were making fun of one of her best friends because she was gay.

I asked her, "Are you saying you don't want to be a Christian—or that you don't want to be judgmental and mean like these kids were?"

"Well, if you're one, then you have to be the other," she replied.

So I asked another question. "If you picture Jesus in the hallway standing right next to Anna while the Christian kids are making fun of her, what do you picture Jesus doing?"

That question got her thinking, and by the time we got home we were both laughing at how awesome Jesus is and that we still want to follow him, but we don't have to be Christians who judge or condemn others. It was a great moment—not because I preached at her, but because the questions enabled her to stand back and think about her faith, who Jesus is, and the kind of Christian she wanted to be.

When our kids are faced with the challenges of their generation—questions around gender identity, sexual norms, or online engagement and addictions—curiosity gives them a lens to discern what Jesus is asking of them in any given situation. Often this comes back to the core beliefs that we've written down as a family manifesto and have lived out together. Your kids might not land quite where you want them to, or it might take them a while and a few mistakes for them to discover the mind of Christ in a particular area, but you've given them tools for discovery that will set them up for a much fuller life as a Jesus-follower.

Apprenticing in the Heart of Christ

Although the mind seems to lead everything, the heart is actually the autopilot of our lives. Sometimes, even without thinking, we make decisions or react to life's circumstances because our hearts are touched, and we just can't not do something. I've always told our kids not to trust their heart, as the Scriptures say it will lead them astray.[5] But the reality is that our heart is a powerful source of movement in our lives, and we have to nurture it so that it beats with the heartbeat of Jesus. Scripture tells us that Jesus wept, he got angry, he got frustrated, and he got sad. The Scriptures also teach that we don't live by law anymore but instead from the inner law inside our hearts.[6] When we move too fast or too deeply, the heart can get us into trouble—but when it is broken and excited for the things Jesus agonizes over and laughs over, it can help form our kids to look more like Christ.

You've probably noticed that this book isn't a manual on how to keep your kids safe. It's more of a manual on developing children who will intuitively live as a poured-out drink offering to the world. And that takes a child with a huge heart.

I have done a lot of weird things over my lifetime, and hundreds—dare I say thousands—of things I lament ... but when I've gotten it right—when I've taken the high road and actually done a good thing—it's always been because of my love for Jesus. Normally there was a vivid moment of mental clarity where I remember thinking, *I would rather not do this, but Jesus would want me to.* As we become more attuned to the thoughts and emotions of Jesus—as we have his heart—we are compelled to do the things he would do. We don't want to live as religious robots or only serve those around us out of duty; we want our motivation to do the right thing to come from a place of compassion, a desire to see justice, and a genuine love of those we serve.

Our kids are growing up in a world where they will face pressure to take the low road, and they will be surrounded by people who will not make choices that reflect the nature of God. The only hope we have is that they will be anchored, informed, and inspired to live large kingdom lives because of a simple love they have for Jesus.

Paul, who endured incredible struggles for his faith, made this clarion call to us all: "For Christ's love compels us" (2 Corinthians 5:14–15). So simple and yet so profound. Moral training is helpful, but it usually fails in time. Doctrinal or theological beliefs are important, but they don't carry the day. Love, however, can sustain a person through the heaviest pressure.

What does it look like to apprentice our kids to grow in the heart of Christ? Here are a few pointers.

Live generously. Jesus modeled generosity in his incarnation, ministry, and death. From giving up his rights as the Son of God, to freely giving his time to those who came to him, to sacrificing his life on the cross, Jesus demonstrated the lavish love of God that withholds no good thing from his children. We often think of generosity in terms of giving financially, but living generously is about being open-handed with our money, time, and effort. Living generously also connects us with the needs of others. Studies show that, from as young as two years old, kids can develop empathy and show compassion. Apparently, this means that they "feel" the other person's pain and they also try to do something to "soothe" them.[7] But in order to show this kind of empathy, a child needs to be aware of another person's discomfort. Those of us living our Metroville lives don't necessarily choose to interact with other people who are obviously distressed—or at least we don't invite them to share about it with us. It's easy for us to be so busy living our own lives, dealing with our own challenges, that we miss the opportunity to connect with others at a level where we can share in their suffering—and maybe even do something about it. So, living generously isn't just about giving to others at arm's length; it's about getting close enough that we can know the needs of others and coming alongside them unsparingly in finding a way through their pain. Recognizing and meeting the needs of others gives our children the opportunity to grow in that compassion. Seeing us, as parents, model compassion in the way that we love on those people apprentices them in how to have the heart of Christ.

Don't avoid suffering. Yeah, sorry. I can't suggest gimmicks for developing a Jesus-heart without some hardship. Ryan suffered terribly with epilepsy, and it crippled every physical, mental, and social part of him, but it only grew his heart. We used to joke about his "thug" persona. He loved to put on bandanas, jewelry, and other things he saw gang bangers or WWE wrestlers wearing because he loved to be tough. And even though he was ninety pounds at his heaviest, he was in more brawls than Bad, Bad Leroy Brown. Why? Because he was always sticking up for someone, especially if they were being made fun of. He was also the most thoughtful member of our family. He seemed to notice the people around us that needed a bit of encouragement, or a gift, or a pat on the back. Something about his suffering built him into what we called the "spiritual patriarch" of our family. He led our family all over the country to new places, new experiences, new relationships, and new exploits. So, although adversity might seem like something we want to ensure our kids never experience, it can be the very thing that grows them into incredibly compassionate, big-hearted, justice-seeking followers of Jesus.

Alli is our rescuer—saving stray animals, orphans, plants … just about anything that needs saving. McKenna is our fighter—advocating for broken kids who have been abused, misused, or thrown on the streets. More than anything else, suffering has been the crucible for what we've all become and now do together, and in that sense has been one of God's greatest gifts to us as a family.

Don't lament hard times. Begin to truly understand what Scripture means when it tells us to "consider it pure joy" when we "face trials of many kinds" (James 1:2). If we choose to shun the human instinct for comfort and security, and instead live a life of generosity, we may find that suffering is a natural byproduct.

When you lean into opportunities to suffer, to advocate for the poor, you're laying the groundwork for unique traits of Jesus to form in your kids' hearts. If you don't let fear get in the way, they will become generous—and they'll make you uncomfortable in how they spontaneously give their money, time, and lives to others. You will also notice that they will advocate and become activists who are willing to resist violent, unjust, and crippling evils in the world. You'll watch in amazement as they carry more weight than the average person; they'll take pay cuts and choose careers that are far less lucrative, just to help people.

Do I wish their hearts weren't so big? Of course I do because I hate to see their hearts hurt. But big hearts celebrate well, laugh big, and cry hard at the right time over the right things. Watching our kids' hearts grow, and seeing them become people who others simply want to be around, makes this mother's and father's heart grow big, too—and we wouldn't change a thing.

Apprenticing in the Hands of Christ

Once, as I was heading through customs in the Eastern Bloc, the border guard looked at my passport and read my last name. "Halter," he said. "Ah … Halter, the one who lifts."

I resisted my normal inclination to keep moving and said, "What did you say about my last name?"

"Halter," he said. "I know that name, and it is a people who are known for lifting heavy things."

This was a life-defining moment for me. My father, Leo Herman Halter, was the hardest working man I ever knew. As a lad, I worked for his roofing company. Watching him lift two full bails of shingles up a rickety old ladder in the ninety-degree sun, hour after hour, left quite an impression. I didn't know just how much until years later. I now even have a tattoo on my right arm that says *ora et labora* (Latin for "pray and work"). It's become the mantra of my life, and it is how others have perceived me over the years as well. *Ora et labora* is a sixth-century saying of Saint Benedict, who started the Benedictine tradition. The Benedictines were the first ones to say that there is really no distinction between the sacred and secular space. The act of prayer and intercession in the world is an act of work, and to work is to pray. Everything is considered sacred, and from the fall of Adam and Eve onwards, our most sacred contribution in the world—our form of living worship—is to work to make the world better.

When we think about what defines, or what will define, our kids, we can't just influence their heart and their mind; we also have to apprentice the work of their hands for Christ.

Working with our kids is the best way to get them to enjoy work. From the age of three, Alli always loved to go to Home Depot with me. It was like it was built into both of us. And when we got home, she'd be all excited to join me in whatever project we were shopping for. Yes, working with Alli made every project much slower, but I think having her with me—letting her try to drill a screw in, hammer a nail, sweep a floor, measure a line, or take a ten-minute coffee and snack break—all contributed to her now being the hardest worker I've seen. She raises two of her own kids, fosters two other children that they hope to adopt, has started a photography studio and a cut-flower farm—and that's just this year!

Consider how formative it can be if your kids grow up loving to work with Mom and Dad, where they can see a job accomplished, witness a product or service being of help to a neighbor, feel the thankfulness and gratefulness of people you serve with your hands. And then imagine if the "work" is considered central to their growing faith and to what it means to be the church of Jesus.

As I mentioned earlier, in Alton we received the gift of a boarded-up building (once the town's post office). Our entire family worked with our hands to renovate the space, get it breathing, and then open it to the public as a coffee shop with a number of other business ventures running out of it as well. Although we do have occasional worship gatherings, our day-to-day prayer is to find things that God wants to fix, build, renovate, and start that benefit our city. Proverbs 11:10 says that "When the righteous prosper, the city rejoices." This is our communal calling, and as all of our kids grow up doing these works together, they'll pick up on the hands of Jesus.

One business that is a part of the kingdom ecosystem in our area is SoulCraft. It was started by a man named Stan, who left his head pastor position at a local church and joined our missionary band. He had a dream of helping young men in Ferguson, Missouri, learn a new identity through work. He now has a retail wood shop on the main street in town. Hanging on the wall of the studio are four symbols that represent how he specifically disciples the hands of Jesus. When young men come in off the streets and start their apprenticeship with Stan, he teaches them to build something that represents each of these four symbols. These are: something to keep (to remind them of a job well done); something to sell (to remind them that their work is worth something); something to give away (to remind them of how other people have given to them); and something to help someone else learn a craft (to remind them that they can apprentice others).

This is such a great picture of true apprenticeship. Yes, he's teaching them a skill, but Stan is also pointing the men he works with back to something more than the products they are making. He's reminding them of the core beliefs he wants them to know for themselves.

One final thing to reiterate: Focusing on the head, heart, and hands is not meant to be a to-do list or a checklist. They are aspects of the life of Jesus that we want to see our kids take ownership of. It's possible you could work all these into a system, but your children could completely miss the *posture* of Jesus. Make sure you encourage your kids to see that living out the head, heart, and hands of Christ is about imitating the physical, human way that Jesus walked on earth. That will help your kids be more apt to walk in the world as he did.

FREEDOM TO FAIL

The last thought on intentionally developing the head, heart, and hands of Jesus is simply to create an atmosphere where failure in any of these areas isn't met with legalism, punishment, or belittling. Nothing shrivels up the life of Jesus in a disciple more than fear and condemnation. That's why 2 Corinthians 3:17 says, "Now the Lord is the Spirit, and where the Spirit of the Lord is, there is freedom."

Discipline, warnings, and letting our kids' sins naturally hurt are all part of helping them grow up and mature in Christ. Delaying gratification, discipling their flesh, and honest pain over missteps is healthy. But developing kingdomlings is more about saying yes and giving them the courage to try, fail, and follow their growing heart to make a difference in the world. Perhaps there's no better example of letting your kids try, fail, and be responsible for their own lives and failures than the story of the prodigal son.[8] The son thought he was ready to venture out on his own, and so the father let him go. And he didn't just release him; he let his son take his inheritance in one of the most brazen acts of disrespect that was known in their culture at the time. The father knew it was time to give his son the freedom to make his own decisions, even if those decisions resulted in failure. And when the young man realized he couldn't handle the freedom, the father didn't disown him, or humiliate him, or admonish him. Instead, the father was there, waiting on the porch to welcome his child home, running to him with open arms as he saw him approach. The son's change of heart was enough for the father—he was more concerned with lavishing his son with love than reprimanding him for the mistakes he made.

My biggest encouragement in discipling your kids is that you be their biggest fans, speak courage, be willing to give them opportunities that will stretch and grow them, and be ready to welcome them with open arms when it doesn't all go to plan.

IN SUMMARY

- Following Jesus isn't about teaching head knowledge; it's about apprenticeship—learning while doing.

- Our responsibility is to form all of Jesus in our kids, and this is what helps Jesus come alive for them.

- Western non-participatory discipleship can shrivel the heart. We discover joy when we give things a go rather than learning more information.

- Forming Jesus in our kids happens in three key areas:

  - Head: having the same focus as Jesus and viewing the world as he does (moving from unbelief to belief, so we need to know what we actually believe).

  - Heart: allowing our hearts to break over the things that break Jesus' heart.

  - Hands: embodying the good news of Jesus and doing his work on earth.

- Developing Jesus in our kids needs to come with a good dose of freedom to fail.

SOMETHING TO THINK ABOUT

- What is your current understanding of discipleship? Is it more about growing in head knowledge or learning as an apprentice?

- Do you see the responsibility to disciple your children as resting on you, or on paid ministry staff?

- How might you begin to apprentice your kids in the head, heart, and hands of Jesus?

- Who in your wider faith community is walking alongside your kids? How might they be involved in apprenticing them in these areas?

- Do you give your kids freedom to fail? How do you respond to them when they do fail?

MAKE IT HAPPEN

- As a parent, you might not feel confident in how *you* are personally growing in the head, heart, and hands of Jesus, let alone your kids. Spend some time thinking about how you might step out and grow in your own discipleship. Then consider how you might share this or allow your kids to see what God is doing in you.

- Consider how you might encourage your kids to grow in some facet of each of the three areas of head, heart, and hands. For example:

  ○ Offer to read the Bible with them, or a book that encourages them in following Jesus.

  ○ Ask them to consider a peer at school who is often sidelined. What is God's heart for that person, and how could kindness be shown?

  ○ Invite them to work with you on a household project, cooking a meal for someone, or mowing the lawn for a neighbor.

From McKenna

As I sit and reflect on our family's life on mission, perhaps what sticks out to me the most has been our family's devotion to taking on hard things in life. I grew up watching my parents make decisions to walk toward, rather than away from, hardship. Of course, we fail and are far off most of the time, but this has shaped how I found my calling in social work, as well as how I hope to engage as a friend and a parent for the community we have found in Alton. Doing hard things has certainly taken on new and deeper meaning since becoming a mom in 2020. Throughout my pregnancy, my husband and I discussed the racial awakening happening across our country, as we would be welcoming a biracial son into the world. What I have learned from my parents, and what my husband and I talk about often, is how we can walk toward this fear rather than running from it. While it would probably be easier to shelter our family from the pain and brokenness of our world, that is not where Jesus is leading us as a family. So, we will continue to follow him into hurting places and take on hard things, with the support of our family and our community who walk with us in these spaces.

6

FINDING YOUR GROOVE

The previous chapters have been about defining the values we have as a family—but what does it look like to put them into practice? All families have practices (even if you can't name them), and we all have routines (even if we think we're laid-back and disorganized). You get up, you go to school/work, someone cooks, you eat dinner; you might have extra-curricular activities through the week; you take vacations at certain points during the year; you celebrate birthdays, weddings, and other milestones. These are all rhythms of family life, but they're more than just things that we do. They speak of our values, and—whether we like it or not—they embed those values and practices into our kids' experience. Kids come to expect those routines. And when they become adults, they often mirror the routines from their childhood. (That's why newlyweds often have an interesting time figuring out their routines together!)

Rhythms can play an important role in helping our kids follow Jesus. When we establish healthy rhythms and consistent practices, our kids begin to grow in the values that undergird those practices.

If you think this invitation to a missional life of following Jesus is total chaos and recklessness, then hear me now: Kids need consistency. Yes, they need adventure, and they need to experience discomfort, but they also need the consistency that comes with following Jesus—what we call "faithfulness." And embedding faithfulness in your kids' lives looks like practicing the principles of following Jesus in everyday life.

I am often asked if there's a way to find balance in raising kids into mission. No! You'll never find a harmonious balance to this life. But you won't find that if you decide not to go on mission either. Life doesn't work in balance; it works in cycles and rhythms. Like the seasons, the tides, or the holidays, we have to focus more on living into the natural rhythms life gives us. Some seasons are easier, and some are harder. At each stage or season, we need to ask God what it looks like to live out our missional adventure as a family: What are the opportunities? What are the restrictions? What does God seem to keep interrupting us with? What are the one or two things we can do together as we grow in having the head, heart, and hands of Christ? Who can we go on the adventure with? As a family, how are we good news to those around us? What resources do we have to serve others?

Right now, we have mostly mid-twenty-somethings in

our community. They all have toddlers ... and lots of them. These families started off barely breathing, struggling to find any energy or space for others while they figured out how to be parents of newborns. Now they've learned to help each other out. They call on one another for "child sharing" (which is essentially giving each other breaks), and some live so close to each other they can meet on porches after the kids are in bed and keep their monitors on from across the street.

Each season of parenting brings with it different challenges as you seek to raise kingdomlings, and it's important to know which season you're in and how to embrace God's calling to you for where you're at.

Infants and toddlers. At this stage, your job is to survive! Pool resources and pay for babysitting together. Whenever possible, try to live close enough so you can put the kids down and still enjoy some adult conversation. You are laying foundations for your little ones to know consistent, unconditional love that mirrors the Father's heart. Guess what? That takes quite a lot of energy, patience, and emotional reserves! Don't expect too much of yourselves, and find ways to get your own downtime.

This is also a good season to simply and consistently plant the seeds of the gospel in your children's lives. Pray over them out loud, so they get used to hearing you talk to God. Tell them about the love of Jesus. Start planting seeds. Something will grow someday.

Elementary age. Include your kids in everything. When you go to help someone on your street, take them along and tell them why and what you're doing, and then thank them for being the church or helping people feel the love of God. Keep communicating in both word and action that the church is more than an event or a place to go. When you gather together for meetings, the older children can watch the younger kids, or you can look for other ways for them to join in so that they don't feel pushed out of the action with the grownups. Give them every opportunity you can to serve and contribute. Get them washing up, preparing meals, picking up litter on your street, going on prayer walks. Start reading the stories of Scripture with them. Speak of other people in your community as examples of what they read in Scripture, so they know it is doable to live that way in real life.

Middle school. This isn't just a time for kids to be awkward and weird; this is when they enter adulthood. In Jewish tradition (the one Jesus grew up in), the age of twelve was when a young man or woman was invited to be like the bigs. Middle schoolers can learn and memorize Scripture and be invited to live into all the things of God. Build deep character traits of truth, servanthood, humility, generosity, and peacemaking. This is the time to talk about everything—no subject should be taboo. They and their friends are going through incredible instability, facing questions about their identity, struggling with what they see on TV and the internet. They are likely to be exposed to pornography and harmful social media, and are dealing with some pretty heavy life stuff.

In our neighborhoods there are a lot of fatherless children, and they've seen more in ten years than most of us see in a lifetime, so they need encouragement at every level. There should be openness and freedom for them to discuss whatever is on their mind. In this season, you are praying and guiding them into stability, their identity in Christ, and regularly calling them into mission. At this age, it's crucial that young people have mentors and role models from within the wider Christian community, so look out for and encourage those relationships in their lives.

High school/college. If we've made it this far as parents, we might expect that our kids would be partners in the gospel at this stage. But we all know that sometimes it just doesn't work that way. We might hope that our kids will be taking part in our shared mission, but sometimes they want nothing to do with anything that involves Mom or Dad. You might even feel like it's too late because you've only just started thinking about discipling your kids. But one honest word really can make up for years of missionary neglect. Your kids don't need anything other than authenticity—a forthright talk about your faith and your doubts. They need to hear the stories of where you've done well, but even more they need to hear the stories of where you've fallen short. You don't have to grovel at the feet of your failures, but with some levity, make fun of yourself and admit the times you were too judgmental with them and their friends, too afraid of trusting them, or too legalistic or religious.

As I mentioned in the previous chapter, give them some freedom to fail. Soon they're going to be off into the world on their own, so now is a good time to let them make some mistakes and learn how responsibility and consequences work. If you're there in the background, like the Prodigal's father with arms open wide, they'll be much better prepared to make that step into adulthood.

For Cheryl and me, the most important thing we passed on at this stage was that we wanted to "talk it over" with them. Whether it was about partying with their friends, booze, drugs, sex, tattoos, activities, traveling without us, or anything else that came up, we'd simply say, "Hey, tonight let's get some time to talk it through." As we did this consistently, our kids learned that we weren't talking at them or down to them but instead talking everything through to help them feel confident in their decisions. The talk gave us time to ask, "How do you feel in your heart about it? Any sense of how Jesus is influencing this decision? What selfish motives are you struggling with in it? Does it feel like a choice between two good options or two bad options? What could go wrong if you do this? Are you okay living with the consequences? What are you learning about yourself in this?"

When we make the time to have even just one significant conversation with our kids each week, it can have a huge impact on them over their lifetime—and not just when they're at home with us. As they then move on into adulthood, you've not only made sure they know they can still talk to you about anything, but you've also given them the tools to make better decisions as adults.

I'm not pretending that living this kind of a life as a family is going to be easy. But there are ways for you to embrace the season you are in, so that you can embody God's call to seek his kingdom in a way that's appropriate to where he's got you.

In the previous chapter we looked at how to help our kids grow in the head, the heart, and the hands of Jesus. Let's now look at four rhythms that will not only help you apprentice them in growing in the head, heart, and hands of Jesus but will also create a living story that your kids will most likely want to emulate and grow into as they mature and leave the nest.

OPEN TABLE

Over the years, I've had the privilege of training missionaries across the globe, and the one consistent rhythm I always tell them to start with is to simply sit down and eat a meal with people. Food is one of the few things that crosses every social, spiritual, and personal barrier. If you look at the lifestyle and rhythms of Jesus, you can basically chart his journey through all the meals he had with people. If he hadn't taken his disciples for a dinner at the home of Levi, a hated tax collector, we wouldn't have the Gospel of Matthew in the Bible.[1] If he hadn't gone to a wedding and saved the party by turning water into wine, we would have missed out on an amazing miracle.[2] And if, on his last night, he hadn't shared a meal with his disciples and asked them to do the same thing by eating often together and remembering him, we wouldn't have the sacrament of the Lord's Supper.[3] (And by the way, the sacrament isn't just a religious time to take a stale wafer and dip it in cheap wine; the sacrament is meant to be a time to eat together and to remember Jesus in the process.)

What would it look like if meals were a time your kids always looked forward to—an anchor for their day?

The table is where we can drop encouragement and wisdom at breakfast, where a quick catch-up can happen at lunch, and where the tired, stressed-out souls of our kids can be renewed at the end of a day. As a family, we would sometimes simply do a "thumbs up, thumbs down" conversation, where the kids would share one lousy thing that happened and one good thing from their day.

But our table times aren't just meant to be for the nuclear family. The more open your table is, the better the experience. When they were growing up, our kids knew that Mom and Dad loved to meet their friends, and they often saw us having our own friends over, too. That meant that our table was often full! But it wasn't always just a way to be social; it was a way to invite others into our life and to show our kids that we were always thinking about others—and it instilled an evangelistic heart in them as well.

For special meals—like Thanksgiving, Christmas, or Easter—our kids watched their mom put an egg, or a seasonal gift, on every place setting, which usually included spots for about ten friends who didn't have another place to go for the holidays. Cheryl would find out who was coming and make sure everyone had their own small gift with the name of each person on it. And our kids got to watch people's responses when they discovered they were not just an afterthought but a valued part of our meal and family. At Thanksgiving we always held a huge football game, and during the downtime of Christmas break, we always had large game nights with thirty people jammed on the floor together, enjoying life and laughter.

You might be reading this and thinking, *I sure don't have room at my table to have ten friends over!* Maybe you live in an urban area where real estate is at a premium and your two-bedroom apartment doesn't have space to swing a cat. But here's the thing: Sharing your table doesn't have to look like cooking up a banquet with caviar and silverware. It could be a simple meal of soup and bread, or it could be a potluck dinner where everyone contributes and you get some help with the washing up, too. It doesn't even have to be around your table. It could be a meal out at a diner or a picnic in the park. Really, it's just about the meal that we share together, the time we spend, and the connection that this grows between us and others.

When we begin to meet with people from different walks of life, there's also something special about seeing the kinds of food that they like to eat. Letting them share their food with us often brings a deeper connection as we find out their story and get to know them better.

In our home—regardless of the type of meal, or who was there—the important thing was that it was a place of levity, of relief, and a time where everyone felt that they were known and loved. Sometimes we'd pray; at other times we just did a meaningful toast, so that folks didn't feel forced into our faith. But whether we prayed together or not, the table was often the place where people felt comfortable to open up about what was happening in their lives. When we think about discipling our children, the table can often be the place where those significant conversations can more easily happen. And when we do that with people we've invited to sit around our table, we become something of God's family, together.

So, who could you invite to your table? When Jesus sent out the seventy-two in Luke 10, he told them to greet people and see who their peace rested on.[4] This is a great principle for us as we seek to connect with and welcome others—who are your people of peace? Who seems open, responds to you, and is willing to accept the invitation? And who is God leading you to? Is it the family next door, or the mom at school who's new to town? Is it the work colleague no one likes? Is it the retired neighbor, whose family lives across the state?

OPEN HOME

This may not seem like a rhythm, but after thirty years of marriage and twelve homes (do the math on that), we've had a consistent rhythm of renovating our home to be the front door of mission. Just like the local pub (short for "public house"), we've always felt that creating warm, inviting places for people to gather is essential. It also seemed to be why people were always coming to us to share about what was happening in their lives. They knew our house was open.

One of the most important attributes of the early Christians was that they showed hospitality to strangers. Hospitality actually means "love of stranger." It means sharing food, sharing rooms, keeping people safe from harm, and extending the same love to others as you would give your own kids. This was not just Jesus' way of teaching us how to be good people; it was his primary strategy for reaching the whole world. When he said that the greatest commandment is to love God with everything you have and to love your neighbor as yourself,[5] he was giving his army the war-room strategy for bringing God's kingdom to earth. It wasn't just about having a nice meal with your lifelong Christian, Bible-study friends; it was a strategy for sharing faith with non-believers. Think about the context: In the time of the early church, it wasn't always safe to be with friends out in public. Persecution was rife, and Christians lived with the threat of being outed and then imprisoned or killed. So instead, the home, or the *oikos*—the extended family— became the way people explained the love of Jesus by sharing everything they had and demonstrating what the family of God was really like.

The point here is really just about making space for people in your life and in your home. Now that we've moved into running a coffee shop in Alton, we've learned that space-making is a new form of evangelism, where many people begin their journey with Jesus. Sometimes people come into

Post Commons and look around at all the improvements and renovations we've made to an abandoned building, and they start to cry. Some ask if I'm the owner, and when I say yes, they just give me a big hug and thank me for making a space for our town to meet and find friends.

That's the power of your home. When you create a space for people, they feel welcomed and wanted; they feel invited to belong.

So how can you make this kind of space for people? Here are a few ideas:

Start with what you've got. Ryan's epilepsy kept us pretty broke, so we initially just did a few simple things to make our home more welcoming. We painted walls warm colors, or we pruned trees back so we could make a small outdoor seating area. As we got a little more into it, we began opening up rooms by demolishing walls that weren't necessary. In one of our houses we finished a basement, so we had a great place for kids to play when we'd invite other families over. On our four-acre ranch in Denver we installed fire pits around the property and turned the barn into a saloon. And now, on our eighty-acre farm in Alton, our daughter Alli is continuing the story by making a homestead full of event spaces that people can rent out, amidst flower gardens, barns, pools, creeks, Airbnbs, and anything she can use to create a place people want to be.

You might live in a small space, or your home might be a rental property and you're therefore limited in the home improvements you can make. But there are still ways you can make your space welcoming. Even some comfortable chairs or beanbags can make people feel at home. Add candles for atmosphere and blankets for when it gets cold. Or simply take the time to have a good selection of hot and cold drinks so that people know you want to be able to give them their favorite herbal tea or the oat milk they prefer.

We live in a culture that tells us our home is our castle, and any renovating we do is just about our own individual wants and needs. We often see home as our safe space where we can enjoy our privacy and downtime. But what if we instead saw our homes as a resource to be shared? Opening our homes is really about opening our lives to people. We need to make space so that they can be listened to and cared for; so that they can join in with the things we're doing and be discipled along the way.

Think about how you can "recycle time." As I already said, our homes and family lives have natural rhythms of mealtimes, routines, chores, and relaxation. Chances are, if you're an active family, your schedule is full of weekly classes, clubs, and social events. And these often run on a rhythm of weekly, monthly, or seasonal rotation. So, opening your home and inviting people into your lives is easy when you make it part of your normal rhythms and routines. What are you already doing that you could invite other people into? It might be a family movie night or a trip to the local park. It might be a Saturday morning walk or another activity you do regularly. We've already talked about having an open table; mealtimes are a great natural rhythm. We all need to eat, and we all generally spend a fair amount of time working on meals for our family. So why not bring others into that? Maybe you pick one night a week when you invite another family to have food with you. Ask if a couple of your kid's friends from their sports team want to come for food before training. Include a neighbor in your Saturday morning brunch.

Set expectations. The idea of an open home can be pretty intimidating for some people—and I get that! I've already told you I'm an introvert, so having people around all the time can drive me a little crazy. We all know what it's like to invite someone over and have them still chatting away at midnight. We want to make living this missional life sustainable, so we're going to have to set some expectations.

This process is the same as setting expectations and boundaries within your own family. If you've welcomed people into your home, it's okay to ask, "Who's gonna help me clear up?" It's okay to set boundaries like, "We're gonna put the kids to bed at 8, so we'll need to have everyone leave then." If someone rings your door, it's okay to say that you need some space: "We're actually in the middle of an argument here, so it's not a good time, but we'll catch up with you tomorrow." People might even appreciate the insight into your less-than-perfect life!

Think about what you need to stop, start, or change. As I've said a few times throughout this book, we can all be in danger of filling our schedules with our Metroville activities.

Living this kind of life as a family can't just be an extra thing you add into your already busy schedules. So, think about what things you need to change or even stop doing in your current routine that will make space to allow you to invite other people in.

How could you create a rhythm that makes sharing life with others a part of your family routine? Could you start by having one night a week that's an "open house night" for your kids to have friends over? Or could you designate a weekend each month when you invite over neighbors, local families, or work colleagues for a party? Could you cut out one of your existing commitments and spend an evening each week where you help with childcare for another family?

Creating a rhythm of opening our homes—and opening our lives—can be one of the most important things we do as a family in our mission to bring God's kingdom. If you continue to make space in your schedule and in your home for people to gather, I guarantee it will make a difference in the lives of those you welcome in.

OPEN BOOK

Most of you "old" people will remember the days when your high school teacher would allow you to take an "open book" test instead of a normal test. The normal tests had you head down by yourself, working the problem, whereas the open book test gave you the opportunity to check your answers in the textbook. In its best variation, you could pick a few friends, go home, order pizza, and stay up late, working the answers together. Of course, everyone loved the latter option because it ensured success, and quite frankly it was a lot more fun.

When you think about our approach to spiritual formation in the past, it mostly included a lot of church services, Bible studies, and, if you were alive in the eighties and nineties, the personal devotional. Looking back, I never really liked any of it, especially if I was by myself or staring at someone who was talking to me as if I were in a lecture. It's been proven that didactic teaching alone is a largely ineffective form of learning, and it's even less effective at bringing about any genuine transformation. Studies show that we only retain 5 percent of what we learn in a lecture.[6] Thus, lectures, sermons, studies, and private devotional reading may serve some purpose, but if we're honest, most of us need learning environments that transform our lives and change us at our core.

Jesus had only three years to turn a bunch of regular, blue-collar workers into a juggernaut of strategic, prayerful, wise world-changers. So how did he do it? And what would you call his method of spiritual formation? Well, I'd call it action/reflection learning. It's Jesus' equivalent of a daily open-book exam.

Whether it was stealing a nap before calming a whitecap storm on the sea of Galilee, or taking his disciples across the lake to the badlands of the metropolis to encounter a cave-dwelling crazy man, or taking a longer route through Samaria so they'd come in contact with a woman by a well, or telling them that today's learning will be to go two-by-two into the city with no provisions—every day had an action, followed by time to reflect, process, ask questions, and learn amidst a community of friends.

This was the way God was going to build his church. In fact, this pattern of action/reflection was literally the life of the church. In our time, we've lost the head, heart, and hands of Jesus in the story because we've assumed that going to church and getting our kids to stay in church will do the trick. But it hasn't. In fact, the fastest growing religious segment in our faith culture is what is known as the "dones." These are people who have put in their time with the church and have found that it just doesn't hold for them. Our young people are the largest group exiting the church.[7] So is Sunday church the problem? No. It's never bad for Christians to gather with other Christians to worship and hear teaching. The problem is that we have unrealistic expectations of what that hour and a half we spend each week "at church" can deliver.

As we explored in chapter three, we have to remember that, for Jesus, the gospel wasn't the good news about the church. He came proclaiming the good news of the kingdom of God[8]—that God's reign was coming to bind up broken hearts, set captives free, and bring comfort to those in mourning.[9] The gospel was about this kingdom of God coming on earth, through Jesus, and his church was how the kingdom was going to be proclaimed and lived out. The goal of the kingdom is not that people simply go to church; the goal is that the people of

God live out God's kingdom and, as they do, he will build his church.[10]

So, when we think about spiritual rhythms for our kids to grow them in their faith, don't immediately try to figure out how to get your kids to go to church and stay in church. Instead, think of ways for them to *be* the church, and stay in the conversation with them along the way. It's a show-and-tell game not a tell-and-tell-some-more game.

You can either instruct your kids to pray every day, or you can put them into situations where they are desperate to pray. You can pressure your kids to behave perfectly, or you can use each misstep to let them figure out the benefits of following Jesus and taking greater and greater ownership as they learn what life is like under the kingdom or under the world's systems. You can urge them to give 10 percent to some nebulous fund, or you can ask them to keep their antenna up for the needs of people and then encourage them to be generous.

The Bible is exactly what it says it is: powerful, double-edged, and sword-like. But the way we've separated it from real life and hoped that learning Bible verses would make world-changers is myopic. It doesn't account for the fact that the presence of God and Jesus through the Holy Spirit is also the living Word. If we keep the Bible in the church, it will be a closed book; but if we let out the life of Jesus, then we'll experience the joys of an open book and true spiritual formation for our kids.

A few years ago, a member of the congregation in a church I was pastoring came up to me and challenged me to preach a

stronger, harder-hitting message, instead of all the "fluffy stuff."
As I'd heard this a few times before, I was ready to respond
and I calmly said, "I appreciate the challenge, so here's what
I'm willing to do. Jesus taught a concept which I call *knowses*,
which means that the only Scripture you really know to the
core of your being is the Scripture that you obey." He nodded,
as if he already knew this and I was wasting his time. "So, do
you know the name of your neighbor yet?"

Somehow he missed my setup and said, "Yeah, I think it's
Kevin … uh, but I'm not sure of his wife's name."

I pressed a little. "What about your neighbors in the other
six houses right around your home? Have you met them yet?
Do you know any of their names?"

"Well, I know those people," he replied, "but I don't really
hang with them. One couple is gay, and the others just aren't
into what I'm into."

"Well, I'm glad you were honest with me on that because I'd
like to suggest that you haven't yet learned the 101 of following
Jesus, and for some reason you've not obeyed him on one of
his most important commands to love your neighbors as much
as your own family. When you can tell me that you've reached
the point of real knowing on that 101, then we can give you
some deeper teaching. But since you're still wading around in
the shallow end, I've got to keep giving you shallow teaching."

Hopefully you see the point. Church and sermons, when
separated from obedience, can become more of a problem than
a help. If you put into practice what you know—loving God and

your neighbors—then worship gatherings and sermons and all the other bells and whistles can serve and augment, but nothing is as powerful as the rhythm of taking action and then reflecting on what we've learned and tried.

My conversation with that member of my congregation was another great example of why going on this journey with others is vital, because sometimes we need other people to lovingly point out our blind spots—the things we don't really "know." As you think about your own "open-book" rhythm, think about who you are learning with. Who is alongside you as you act in obedience to Jesus? It might be those you already know in your church community or small group. It might simply be another family who also want to learn how to disciple their kids and follow Jesus in his mission. When we live out obedience to Jesus together, there's a powerful opportunity for Jesus to build his church right where we are.

OPEN ROAD

This last rhythm might seem a little strange, but we've got to go there. One of the greatest life-changers is to see other places, learn about other people's stories, and, in the process, learn to appreciate what "home" means. Both our girls traveled the world, and it changed them. On one trip, I took McKenna (then age thirteen) on a long drive through downtown Detroit. At the time, Detroit was a bombed-out city, and that one drive is still etched in my memory as a special time when we talked about poverty, violence, love, and what our family was about.

On another trip, we sent Alli by herself to work in one of the poorest barrios* in the world, in a literal dump in Nicaragua, and we sent McKenna with a small team to Africa. Both trips were when the girls were about fifteen or sixteen. These short weeks abroad did more for our girls than ten years of Bible studies or sermons.

Friends of mine have chosen to take their family on a two-week trip to India every few years. This isn't just missional tourism; they make the sacrifice to do this instead of their vacation at a nice beach resort. They stay in an orphanage and get involved in farm work and helping with basic chores. It's given their kids the opportunity to see the reality of how over a quarter of the global population lives. My friends would say it's given their kids a different perspective on the privileged lives they lead. Now when they're asked to load the dishwasher at home or do some laundry, it's no longer a big deal. They've seen a bigger world and have a bigger perspective.

These kinds of experiences don't necessarily have to come through long-distance trips. There are people facing difficulty in every town and city in the world. Other friends of mine have chosen an open road nearer home. Each week, together as a family, they serve at a sit-down meal for the homeless and vulnerable of their city. It means their kids are used to chatting

---

* A barrio literally means a "quarter" or "neighborhood" of a city in Spanish, but generally means an area where most people live in significant poverty and deprivation.

with people who don't fit in the middle-class box, and this has helped them build awareness and compassion for the needs of people around them.

Pointing our kids to the bigger story that we're living and the bigger world that we're part of is a great way of counteracting the narrative of Metroville that tells them their lives are for their own pleasure and comfort. And guess what? It's a more exciting story than the one that tells them that being a Christian is simply about following the rules and attending church. Living this bigger story as a family gives your kids a much greater chance of wanting to continue on with their own path of following Jesus. It invites them to really know him and to have the joy of playing a part in seeing his kingdom come on earth.

COUNTERCULTURAL NEIGHBORHOOD CHANGERS

Let me end this chapter with a simple story that happened last Sunday morning at our farm as we celebrated Easter. We hosted a big brunch, with most of the families that serve in our business network or who have found us through the coffee shop or the neighborhoods we live in. It was a full house: lots of toddlers and about forty folks, including a couple of young men who found faith inside our community and two homeless men who are part of our collective church family after one of our families took them in.

As we finished some great food and coffee, we settled into some casual acoustic worship and a simple reading of the Easter Scriptures. Then we prayed and spoke life into Harry, the homeless gentleman we were about to send to a year-long, live-in recovery program in downtown St. Louis. There were lots of tears, laughter, beautiful music. And the kids were not just a side show; they were with us the entire time. Then we had the compulsory egg hunt, followed by another hour or so of everyone around a fire with some spontaneous banjo and guitar playing. Pictures were taken, and there were lots of hugs. And without expressing it in words, most of us knew this time together was what we were all after.

These are our friends who we are living life with, who we share a common mission with, and who all do hard things to help people on the tough side of the tracks. They are the same people we'll see almost every day around our business network or our homes. Everyone lives within two miles of each other, so although Easter Sunday was great, we have similar experiences throughout the rest of the week.

Today, we learned that Harry made it less than twenty-four hours in his new home, and we all stand vigil together for him on his road to recovery. Despite these kinds of knocks, we know we'll keep living this life and mission together. This is church for us. No one is a consumer; we all contribute to this life together.

You can begin something similar in your own neighborhood, regardless of whether your present church experience reflects this. Every church has a mandate to develop and deploy countercultural neighborhood changers, but you don't have to wait for your pastor or church staff to program it for you. Your mandate is from the Lord, and the place to start is with your own kids and a few friends. The sooner you begin living church, the sooner you'll experience the kingdom, and the sooner you'll see God build his church in the lives of those in your community.

IN SUMMARY

- All families have practices, routines, and rhythms. These speak of our values and imbed those values into our kids.

- At each stage or season, it's important for us to ask how God wants us to live as a family on mission. Different ages and stages might require different ways of living out his call on our lives.

- Four rhythms can help us live as kingdom families:

  o Open Table: eating with others, where people can really share their lives.

  o Open Home: showing hospitality and love to others (Jesus' key strategy for reaching the world).

  o Open Book: learning through action and reflection, in community.

  o Open Road: connecting with people and experiencing places that are far from our reality, giving our kids the opportunity to see the bigger story.

SOMETHING TO THINK ABOUT

- What does it look like to live out a missional adventure as a family in the season or stage of family life you are in?
- What might having an Open Table look like for your family?
- What might having an Open Home look like?
- What might Open Book learning look like in your family and your wider Christian community?
- What might the Open Road look like for your family?

MAKE IT HAPPEN

As a family ...

- Look at your weekly/monthly/yearly schedule. Where are there spaces to connect with others? What might you need to start/stop/change?
- Invite someone you haven't had in your home before to come over (for a movie night, to watch the game, eat takeaway, have a cup of coffee ... anything that makes them feel welcomed and makes it a simple first step for you).
- Consider changing your approach to Bible study and ask the question, "Am I living what Jesus asks me to do so that I really 'know' my Bible?"
- Plan a family trip to a place where people live differently from you. It could be as simple as shopping in a supermarket or going for a coffee in a different part of town. How might your family regularly connect with people from different walks of life?

From Alli

Growing up, our home was never just ours. To some that might sound like the opposite of what they want for their life, and honestly, at times, I felt the same, but it is also the reason my life looks as it does now. There were always people in and out of our home. At any given time, we would have someone—a family or a few people—living with us. People were always drawn to my parents and knew that if they needed a non-judgmental place to heal and grow, they could find it with them. Some of the people I hold dearest, the people I run to for wisdom and guidance, are the same people that ran to my parents for their help. In some ways, the people they poured their lives into became extended family for me.

Fast forward to my current life, and it doesn't look much different; you will often find my home full of children, as my husband and I have been fostering for a little over two years. Although I often wish I could live without the heartbreak of this work, I wouldn't change a thing. For the past five years, our life has been a roller coaster of house moves, job changes, and kids in and out of our home—which is not very different from the past thirty years of my parents' life. I grew up watching them wildly follow God's call, oftentimes leaving behind the "picture perfect" lifestyle that so many people chase after. And now I find myself doing the same.

"Beauty for ashes" (Isaiah 61:3) has always been a strong theme for our family. Whether it be restoring old homes and buildings into thriving centers of communities, opening our home up to others, or simply walking through the ashes of losing Ryan, I've always known and trusted that God will indeed provide beauty along the way. Growing up in this way has helped me to realize that no matter how ugly or how broken something or someone is, if we allow him, God is always ready to provide the sunlight.

When we moved to Alton, my husband, Matthew, was offered a job as a fireman in a town about twenty minutes away. This was a sought-after job in a community which was considered the best place to raise a family. We took the job, bought a house, but within a year, we realized our life, our community, and our calling pointed us back to Alton. So, without hesitation we took a 30 percent pay cut when a job opened up on the Alton Fire Department Squad. Through that, I have learned that the best things in life are not related to money but instead come from being a part of an intentional community of people.

7

BROKEN TREES

A few years ago, when Ryan was twenty-one, I took him to a basketball game he was playing in. To be honest, I wasn't excited to go. I was pooped and wasn't in the mood for a loud gymnasium.

Ryan's team was a mix of developmentally disabled people from fourteen to sixty years of age. Most had Down's syndrome, autism, cerebral palsy, or some other form of physical or mental limitation. Some of them were high functioning, but most were severally impaired, and watching them struggle to talk and walk, let alone play a game of basketball, was pretty tough on the heart.

Imagine the scene: Ryan double-dribbled the ball with both hands all the way down the court, and no one called a violation. After he air balled from twelve feet, someone from the other team threw the ball back so he could try again. Air ball again. This time, another kid took the ball to Ryan and invited him to step a little closer. The players cleared the lane so he could have an open shot. He took the shot, and the ball bounced around the rim but fell to the side. All the players patted him on the back and congratulated him for getting close, and Ryan had a big smile on his face.

Then the other team came down the court. A girl in a wheelchair, pushed by a teammate, had the ball in her lap and was gripping it tightly but needed another person to help hold her head up. The girl pushing the wheelchair could hardly walk herself—she strained to push forward, but her left leg dragged behind her. Once the wheelchair was positioned under the basket, another team member asked permission to shoot on the girl's behalf. He made the shot, and they all gave the girl in the wheelchair a hug, as the shooter unassumingly ran back down to get ready for the next play. This continued until every person got some meaningful experience from the game. All the parents were rooting for everyone, and no one looked at the scoreboard—because no matter what the real score was, the scorekeeper kept the game even. No one was a loser. Everyone had a part to play. Appearance or capacity meant nothing. Everyone was dependent upon each other. No one was ashamed of failure. Everyone was simply thankful for life, and they couldn't wait to see each other at the next game.

Although I never felt excited about going to those games, I always used to drive home feeling like a kid who just got invited to climb over the wall and peer into heaven.

A BEAUTY UNSEEN

This book has laid out a pretty high-bar vision for our children, but I also need to talk honestly about the reality so many families deal with: broken trees.

I got the phrase "broken trees" from a church in Denver by the same name. They are a community almost entirely made up of families who have children with developmental disabilities. I'm not sure exactly why they named the church Broken Tree, but I love the image it evokes. Isaiah 61 speaks of the family of God as "oaks of righteousness" (verse 3). Later in that passage, God prophesies that his family, his people, his church, will someday bring the blessing of God to the world and that their ashes would be turned into beautiful things. I love this Scripture, and the image of a tree, because it lays out an expansive vision of our families—both nuclear and faith families—as a huge orchard or forest united together to change the world ... and that forest includes some broken trees. In fact, *mostly* broken trees.

This may be shocking for you to hear, but most families have some sort of disability in the ranks.

The existence of a "disability" is considered a secondary demographic—the census bureau only recognizes ethnic classifications—so there are really no concrete statistics on the disabled population, which is one of the reasons why this cause is not center stage. Years ago, though, Cornell University published a study claiming Colorado's disabled population was 10 percent.[1]

That statistic accounts for those with physical or developmental disabilities. But if we think about it, we all have some sort of disability, some sort of brokenness, that affects our ability to live the fullness of life Jesus came to bring us.[2] Some of us battle depression or suffer from PTSD or other mental health struggles. Others of us have faced bereavement, or have been physically, sexually, or emotionally abused at some point in life. Some of us have faced neglect or have been orphaned. We may be dealing with drug or alcohol addictions or crippling debt. And then there are those who suffer silently: the kids who live a latchkey life without any real encouragement or wise counsel, who make bad decisions and perpetuate many of the cycles they have experienced; the elderly who feel alone and ignored in a society that expects people to be strong and capable; those dealing with the fallout of family trauma … the list goes on and on. We can end up feeling like we're driving through a forest road after a tornado blew through. Yes, a few trees are standing upright, but most are blown down and laid bare from the high winds of life.

LIFE ON THE RIVER

Every few months I get invited to a game of poker with some local guys. I've learned to plan on losing my $20 every time … yet I keep going back because on occasion I actually win some hands. Like an unskilled golfer who's hungry to keep playing because they manage to hit one or two good shots in an entire round, I get sucked in. I have won some now-infamous games in what is called "the river." This poker term denotes the last card that is turned over that you can use in your hand. In other words, there have been several times I've had a terrible hand but decided to stay in until the last card, and I somehow managed to get the one card that is—impossibly—exactly what I need.

I know there are families that always seem to get the best hand dealt to them. Sometimes I even wonder if God actually puts one in every neighborhood just to tick us off. You know the people I mean. They have enough money, their grass is always green, and instead of hamburgers on the grill they have steak. Their kids are the jocks, the head cheerleaders, and they vacation in Cabo. You know. The perfect people.

And then there are those of us who get dealt what appears to be an unfair hand. We have to work two or three jobs, the medication costs a third of our actual income, it takes thirty minutes just to get the less functional members of our family in the car to go anywhere, we're always behind on house duties, and we're lucky if our kids actually get invited to anything, let alone a prom, or dance, or club.

If the second description pretty much conveys your lot in life, you may have asked yourself these questions: *How do I view the hand I've been dealt? Is it a liability, a straitjacket that limits my enjoyment of the full life? Does it signal that God doesn't really care, or that, even worse, he may not even be real? Surely a loving God wouldn't wish this on anyone he loved.*

Many of those questions and thoughts were my own. That is, until one serendipitous day in New York.

GEORGE REITZ

I was in Queens, New York, for a week, training church leaders and was on my last leg, spiritually, physically, and emotionally. This week, however, would turn out to be one of the most defining weeks of my life. Just before I left the training venue, I was stopped by a man named George who had been hosting our event. He was a tender Jewish man who was absolutely in love with Jesus and was adored by everyone. I respected him greatly.

"How are you doing, Hugh?" he asked me.

Feeling thankful that he cared enough to ask, I thought, *what the heck!* and proceeded to dump two years of frustration on him: "George, I'm here physically, but I'm dead spiritually. I'm upset with God. He doesn't speak to me anymore, and he doesn't seem to want to really help. My son is having so many seizures, I don't have any energy to paint houses, be a dad or a husband, let alone a spiritual leader. I just don't know how God expects me to serve him without fixing my son."

George didn't say a thing. The sweet smile he had on his face while listening to me turned to a quivering lip. Tears began to roll down his cheeks. He bent over, knelt down on his knees, placed his head on the ground, and, as he put his hands on my feet, he began to pray: "Father, Hugh is having a hard time trusting you because he's tired. He sees Ryan's disability as a limitation. Would you show him the beauty, the power, and the ministry that must now flow from his home, from his weakness, from his brokenness. May he see your power and freedom through these very real constraints."

I don't remember much after that. I don't even remember giving George a hug or saying thanks. I think I was just caught up in that moment of revelation. I had forgotten that God's mission isn't about all we do for God when we're feeling good about things or when we're strong and capable. Instead, God's mission flows from our normal life, as we run with a limp.

The beautiful thing about making the mission of God a family story is that it not only makes room for the broken, but it *assumes* we are broken. Said another way: When you sign up your family to live for God's purposes in the world, brokenness isn't something that hinders mission; brokenness is the bedrock of mission.

WEAKNESS IS POWER

God's world is most certainly an "upside-down" version of our own. What we think brings happiness seems to kill the soul, and what we think hurts us is often critical to our growth. Likewise, there are many strong individuals in Scripture who were weak: Goliath, Sampson, Pharaoh, Herod, to name a few. They looked strong on the outside but crumbled in critical situations. The Apostle Paul was another strong individual, but instead of leaning on his own strength, he used his difficult circumstances to grow his dependence on

God. In 2 Corinthians, Paul spoke of his desire to be rid of an impairment—a "thorn in [his] flesh":

> *Three times I pleaded with the Lord to take it away from me. But he said to me, "My grace is sufficient for you, for my power is made perfect in weakness." Therefore I will boast all the more gladly about my weaknesses, so that Christ's power may rest on me. That is why, for Christ's sake, I delight in weaknesses, in insults, in hardships, in persecutions, in difficulties. For when I am weak, then I am strong.*
>
> 2 Corinthians 12:8–10

Paul is helping us rethink how we view disabilities and brokenness of any kind. Something special happens when we are limited. There's a strength that comes from God when we are frail. God's power actually often shines through our physical sicknesses, emotional instability, and mental anguish.

Getting more specific about the way weakness can be essential for our ministry, Paul says in 2 Corinthians 4:7–12:

> *But we have this treasure [the gospel and ministry of reconciliation] in jars of clay to show that this all-surpassing power is from God and not from us. We are hard pressed on every side, but not crushed; perplexed, but not in despair; persecuted, but not abandoned; struck down, but not destroyed. We always carry around in our body the death of Jesus, so that the life of*

Jesus may also be revealed in our body. For we who are
alive are always being given over to death for Jesus' sake,
so that his life may also be revealed in our mortal body.
So then, death is at work in us, but life is at work in you.

What a great picture—the death and suffering of Jesus being carried and demonstrated in our own physical bodies, showing the life of Jesus to the world.

THE REAL STORY OF THE BIBLE

The second church we started in Denver was called Adullam. It was named after a cave where King David hid—a place where losers hid. *Losers? I thought David was a stud.* Well, he was until King Saul got jealous and started looking for every opportunity to kill him. After that, he lost everything, pretended to be crazy, and hung out in caves, picking scabs and trying to avoid being murdered by his enemies. Eventually, God began to reestablish him, and he met with a band of loyal men in Adullam (which means "refuge"). The scene is described this way in 1 Samuel 22:2: "All those who were in distress or in debt or discontented gathered around him, and he became their commander. About four hundred men were with him." Many scholars believe that the mighty men we later see doing incredible exploits for their king were initially the band of losers we read about here.[3]

After David is back in power, 2 Samuel 9 describes an incredible scene. Once again, David has everything he could possibly want and has the privileges everyone expects a king to have. David asks if there is anyone in Saul's household to whom he can show kindness. The answer is a young disabled boy by the name of Mephibosheth—the son of David's best friend, the late Jonathan. When the boy was five years old, he was accidentally dropped by his nurse and became crippled.

When David has Mephibosheth brought to the palace, the boy bows before David and clearly feels intimidated and unworthy to be before the king.

"Don't be afraid," David reassures him, "for I will show you kindness."

"I am but a dead dog," Mephibosheth responds.

But David has none of it and insists that Mephibosheth will always be cared for and will eat every meal at the king's table.

It's a beautiful story that foreshadows the bigger picture of the gospel—the "good news." It's clear that Mephibosheth feels shame. Imagine the day David's marauders came to summon him. He surely knew that, as a grandson of Saul (David's archenemy), any emissaries from David's court would be there to either hassle or kill him. As this boy stumbled to the door, he most certainly would have not only felt the shame of his family's gaffes with David but also the shame of his disabilities.

Shame can be a prevalent emotion for families with broken trees. We might even be ashamed of feeling shame—but if we're truthful, there are times when our disabilities leave us feeling exposed and vulnerable. Ryan's seizures never tended to come at good times. Often they would happen in supermarkets, ice rinks, on the pews in front of the church, or in crowded restaurants. On rare occasions, Cheryl and I would sneak out for a twenty-minute drive to the ice cream shop, only to return to find him lying in the middle of the road or face down in a pool of blood on a neighbor's porch. Several times we even had people bring him to our home after finding him having a seizure on the sidewalk. Their looks often said it all: "Nice job, parents." And our stories aren't even that bad. Imagine hundreds of thousands of parents of autistic children who blurt out obscenities or guttural screeches every ten seconds, or the violently disabled who live in a mental cocoon of psychosis. You know why you don't see too many of these families in Sunday church services—it's just not worth the emotional effort to try to appear normal. We shouldn't have to feel shame, but when your kids don't fit society's accepted norms of behavior, it can be pretty tough.

Even those of us with less obvious "disabilities" still may feel ashamed of the impact they have on our lives and the lives of others. We may feel we have to present ourselves as polished and perfect in order to be missionally effective and accepted by others. But God is able to build his kingdom in spite of all the chaos we live with. His redemptive purposes are achieved as he weaves his ways through our weaknesses, our dilemmas, our brokenness, our physical limitations, and a cornucopia of distressing situations. His beauty is always there ... but you must look for it.

A BEAUTY TO BEHOLD

I've already shared about watching Ryan's basketball game, but there's another picture of beauty I want you to see: Hallie.

Ryan's girlfriend, Hallie, was born with an undiagnosed impairment that allowed her to perform only basic functions. She and Ryan were perfectly matched and found a sweet friendship and love. Hallie had some difficult seasons, when days and weeks in the hospital were just part of survival.

At one point, Hallie's brain was swelling, leaking, and doing all sorts of other things a brain shouldn't have to put up with. She was in a lot of pain and couldn't lift her arms above her shoulders, but she still managed to text Ryan and ask him to come see her at the hospital. We all drove up together. On the way in, Ryan asked if we could stop at the hospital gift shop and buy Hallie a card. Once inside, he couldn't settle for just a card. He ended up buying her a stuffed animal, a balloon, and some other stuff, all with his own money. Once in her room, we all blushed as we watched the two of them gently comfort one another. Ryan spoke so sweetly, knowing the pain Hallie was in, and she in turn fought off the pain to thank him for coming. As we left, Cheryl whacked me across the arm and said, "You could learn a few things about nurturing from that kid."

It's hard to write this—even now—not because it's sappy, but because it convicts me. You see, we often feel sorry for broken kids and broken families, and even more, we hope for and try to help families not be so busted up. But the reality is that broken people often exhibit God's beauty more than healthy ones do. Sometimes we have to look hard to see it, but it's true. I was convicted hundreds of times by Ryan's generosity and sensitivity, and Hallie's toughness.

Watching kids with Down's syndrome, for example, doesn't have to be sad. If you've ever noticed, most seem to be quite happy, almost 24/7! Seeing kids push their friends in wheelchairs during a basketball game isn't pathetic; it's amazing. Getting to know parents who have spent their last dime buying medication, paying hospital bills and items needed to keep their autistic child alive shouldn't make us feel pity. Their actions show the depth of where love will go. I could go on forever, but I hope you get the point. Our disabilities need to be seen for what they are: the soil in which the beauty of Christ's kingdom is cultivated and grown. Being on mission for God is for the least of us.

Gentleness, acceptance, pure happiness in the moment, generosity, toughness, thankfulness for a good day, perspective on what's important, strength, sense of humor—these are all things that God grows in the hearts of those who can't operate in their own strength.

Even as I'm writing this, I'm sitting at a local Panera restaurant. Through the window, I see a family coming through the front doors. A woman is pushing her husband, who is in a wheelchair. Both arms have metal hooks, and he's got an apparatus that allows him to move a lever that propels the motor on the wheelchair. His young son is holding the door open. The boy's mother is laughing because, as the dad drives his chair through the door, the rubber doormat gets wedged in the axle, and he spins rubber, not going anywhere. Instead of freaking out or angrily pushing him through, she and her son smile. She jumps on the back of the rug and he pulls her through the store, as if she's on a water ski.

Though his disability is severe, they are somehow finding fun together as a family. Sure, there are things this young boy won't be able to do with his dad, but he's also getting a lot—he's getting to see that it's possible to have fun regardless of the circumstances; he's getting to see that the struggles of life don't have to define your ability to experience joy; he's getting to grow up knowing that a person's identity isn't defined by their physical abilities; he's getting to be part of a world where there is care and kindness for everyone, no matter their struggles. I'm pretty sure that boy will someday be anchored in beautiful memories of his childhood that will shape and change the way he sees everything.

Here's the nub of it: Brokenness exposes grace. When we look at the story of King David, brokenness gave the opportunity for grace to break in. It's hard to know if Mephibosheth's disability held any sort of purpose, but when we see it addressed by a graceful king who redeems and offers a place at his table, a beautiful picture emerges. It's through the cracks that the light can shine. And just like David with Mephibosheth, or Ryan and Hallie, or the family at my local Panera—people encounter God's grace and compassion and mercy in the midst of the brokenness of life.

A home full of struggle can make us feel like our family is the last place where the kingdom is breaking through. It can feel like missional living is completely beyond us. Believe me, over the years Cheryl and I were often concerned about how much we could open our home because of Ryan's severe needs. *What happens if Ryan has a seizure? Will his disability make it difficult or uncomfortable for people? Could it be too much for them to handle?*

I guess most of us would feel like this. In high school, my older sister was in the deepest part of her schizophrenia, and there were days when my friends were over and Heidi would be hallucinating about grizzly bears chasing her. Even though my friends knew of her mental disability, the discomfort of watching her run around the house, screaming, and hiding behind chairs, meant I eventually decided I never wanted to invite friends over again. What high school student wouldn't make this decision? As parents, it can feel all too natural to make these sorts of decisions as well.

We all feel pressure to have our houses in order when people come over. We don't just want our homes to be presentable and our food to be palatable—we want the people in our families that way too! So when we're in a season of life when we're struggling, we often make the mistake of quietly closing the doors to our home. I even notice that when young families have their first newborn, they often seem embarrassed by the noises the baby can make—whether it be crying, sucking noises, or the occasional diaper blow out—and many decide simply not to go out and not to let anyone in.

But it's often in the midst of the times where we feel we're not "together" that others can really encounter something of

God's beauty. You'd be surprised at the sense of belonging that is created when people feel you're willing to let them in on your mess. One of my friends once described how her home-based microchurch showed up while she was wiping the walls down from the dinner her toddler had thrown across the table. She initially felt embarrassed, but within minutes they were all joining in with the clean-up and it led to other people in the group being more willing to host—they now know a clean house is not a requirement for welcoming others.

When we let life happen, we can recognize the beauty in all of it.

THE LONG-TERM PERSPECTIVE

For many enduring significant pain and suffering, the only real solace might be to realize that someday we'll see all this through a lens of ultimate beauty. Romans 8:28 says that "in all things God works for the good of those who love him." Good means perfection. Someday, in the heavenly sphere, Cheryl and I will see Ryan in his perfected state, the way God intended him to be. Hallie's parents will see her beautifully adorned with the perfection of Christ, and they will understand their lives in the context of God's purposes. They will smile, knowing God's grace sustained them, and they'll be proud that their lives exposed God to us. And we'll understand, finally and completely, how and what God did through their brokenness. We'll see the lives they touched and the people they pointed to Jesus. We'll see the crucial part they played in making the mission of God a family story.

We are all dealt a certain hand, and at some point, that hand includes people who are not perfectly whole or functional. Whatever the hand holds, God has a unique way of fashioning his story from our story. That moment with George in New York was life changing for me. From that moment on, I stopped trying to fix everything and instead began using our home, inviting people into our lives, and planting churches. Over the years, hundreds of people have sat on our back or front porch, living room or pub room, and we've been able to pour our lives into theirs. And Ryan … he was right in the middle of it all.

Looking back, it's Ryan who has launched our family into everything we've done and are now doing. We live on an eighty-acre farm we call Ry Dog Farm, and Cheryl's equine therapy center is called Rí Beag Refuge. Ryan's thumbprint has been the Lord's way of calling our family into a deeper story, and I hope you can see that brokenness is the very soil from which God creates all our stories.

IN SUMMARY

- This book has laid out a high-bar vision for our kids, but the reality for many families is that we live as "broken trees."

- All of us have some sort of disability, whether seen or unseen. We can choose to view these as the bad hand we've been dealt, or we can see how God actually works through our brokenness.

- Shame can isolate us from community and make us feel unworthy of participating in God's kingdom work, but throughout the Bible, God uses seemingly weak individuals as conduits for his power. It's often when we are limited that God's strength really shines through.

- Broken people often give us a glimpse of God's beauty as we get to see the depth of where love can go. Amid brokenness, people can encounter God's grace, compassion, and mercy.

SOMETHING TO THINK ABOUT

- Look at the hand you've been dealt. What can you thank God for? Where can you begin to ask God to show his strength at work through your family?

- Do you have a sense of shame about your own weaknesses as a family? Why is that?

- What might you learn from other "broken trees" around you?

MAKE IT HAPPEN

- Find a way to spend time with an individual or family impacted by a disability of some sort. Ask God to show you his beauty and power at work through their weakness. Consider how you might learn from and encourage them.

- As you open up your home and your table to others, think about how you can make it accessible and make everyone feel welcome.

- With one or two others, share your own weaknesses as a family and where God is at work in and through those weaknesses.

From Momma Cheryl

When the Lord called our family to Alton, there were way more questions than answers. We knew as a family we were being called, but we did not see clearly why until the summer of 2020. A few years after moving to Alton, Ryan came back home to live with us to try and get his health under control. My focus became very clear—to once again take care of my boy. He was my greatest purpose and our inspiration. Ryan made our family who we are, and, as hard as it was to have him back home, everything felt complete once again. On July 11, 2020, we lost Ryan—the greatest part of our family. His sisters got to spend his last six years on earth with him; his brothers (in law) got to know and love him and create precious memories with him. His niece, Mila (his greatest friend), and nephew, Leo, got to laugh, play, hug, snuggle, and pray, as well as learn about the hard issues of life and death and how Jesus is in the midst of it all. To this day, they talk constantly about their uncle Ry. Ryan was my family's greatest struggle and greatest gift—he was our inspiration, and he was our main calling to Alton. I struggled greatly (and still do) with losing my boy, "my purpose"; and God and I have fought a lot about that. But in God's perfect plan, he was not done with me yet and had still another purpose for me that I would not have taken on if Ry was still here. Ryan's leaving started a journey for me with my horses and for my heart to find some healing. Rí Beag Refuge was born—an equine therapy program for those struggling with trauma—a place where beauty can be found in the ashes and God's heart for the broken-hearted can be shown.

CONCLUSION
STARTING OVER

When Alli was sixteen, we had a particularly infamous battle. She was going through a dark time, and one evening I overheard her being disrespectful to Cheryl. I went and stood in the doorway without saying a word, hoping my presence would calm things down a bit.

It didn't.

In fact, after Alli made a few disrespectful comments aimed at *me*, I told her to stop talking altogether. And then to make the point more dramatic, I decided to slam my hand against the wall on my way out of the room. What happened next surprised even me. I found myself pulling my hand out of the drywall. Apparently I was a bit more enthusiastic than I thought and made a nice hole, right above Cheryl's head. (Remember, she was the one I was trying to protect.)

With that, Alli ran out of the room and locked herself in the car in our garage. As I stood there looking like a big dumb WWE wrestler, Cheryl said, "Nice job. That really helped." She continued, "You'd better go downstairs and fix that with Alli … and after that, you better fix this wall!"

Well, it took five hours to get Alli out of the car—far more time than it took me to fix the wall. And even after I got her out of the car, things were pretty rough for the next three weeks. Alli simply wasn't talking to me. I finally lumbered downstairs to her evil, dark lair. As I sat on her bed, I simply said, "Hey, Dad was a dope, and I'm sorry I went overboard." No, I didn't remind her about her own behavior. I simply took ownership of my side of the problem and said, "Dad is going to try to be much better at listening and helping you through these moments in the future."

With that one little apology, the relationship was restored.

As I've presented the potential of your family living a life of mission together, I know it often raises a lot of concerns about time lost, time wasted, or missed opportunities with our kids. This missional way of life might even be new to you, so how do you make up for not starting sooner? The simple answer is to verbally acknowledge the misses and proclaim a new desire. That's the essence of repentance—turning from one way of thinking and living and going in the opposite direction. Sharing with your kids that you feel challenged to live differently and including them in the conversation will go a long way toward helping them to engage in this new kingdom adventure. It will also model to them that following Jesus always involves being willing to step out and live differently, whatever life has previously looked like.

Hopefully you've gotten this message throughout this book: You don't have to be perfect to lead your family into mission; you just have to be honest and willing to set an example, however imperfect.

SEE WHAT GOD SEES

Vision is the ability to see what God wants and move people toward his desired goal in any situation. If you feel like this book has left you needing to start over with your family, start by seeing what God sees. Start by asking for his vision to be revealed for you, your kids, and your family.

One year, there were eighteen new babies born in our church family. While celebrating one Sunday, I asked if any of the parents had named their baby after a vision they had for their child's life. A handful raised their hands and then proudly shared.

One said, "My grandson was born yesterday, and his name is Cohen, which means 'brave one.'" Cheryl shared that our daughter Alli's name means "raven-haired beauty." You could see the vision the parents had for their children just by the names they had given them.

Of course, there were other parents who looked at each other with a bit of disappointment. One woman even elbowed her husband as if to say, "Way to go, knucklehead. We just named our kid after a stupid TV-show personality."

Well, if that's you, don't be too bummed. Regardless of whether or not you keyed into God's prophetic vision for your children when you named them, the reality is that God has a vision for each of your children, and we can all begin to rebuild a heavenly vision over them as we apprentice them in following Jesus. Holding onto a true biblical vision for their lives will empower you, helping you guide and develop them toward God's vision. It won't just be a wish. You'll have a hand in helping them see what God sees as the bigger story for their lives.

At the start of this book, I was clear that I wasn't trying to help parents who simply wanted to keep their kids in church. The kind of righteous brood we're looking to develop involves much more than church attendance—it's about drawing our kids into a kingdom mission that helps them fall in love with Jesus. If we have that kind of vision for our kids' lives, we're probably on the right track.

For the Halter family, our vision has been defined by the word "faithfulness." We've always desired to be faithful to Jesus in his daily call on our lives. We've tried to live well, wherever he's planted us as a family, and to be faithful with every opportunity. So, whether we're opening our home to others, making a meal for a family in need, or taking time to listen to someone who's having a tough time, we're simply being faithful to what we believe Jesus calls us to do. That's a big enough vision for us.

As our kids grew up, we trusted that the freedom and life of the kingdom they experienced as we lived it out as a family would eventually help them to form their own sense of calling.

I've already told you that Alli, as a young teen, got fed up with being a Christian because of the hypocrisy she perceived in some of the Christians she knew. But she loved it when our church community spent a whole day in the poorest neighborhood of our city. "Dad," she told me, "if this was church every day, I'd be into that." What she was communicating was that helping people, especially the poor, was the "why" for her, at that moment. Through that experience, loving people was no longer just a nice idea, or a concept we talked about in church—it was something she was getting to live out in her life.

Listen to what your kids are communicating to you. What aspects of the good news of Jesus excites them? What are they passionate about? Which Christians do they gravitate toward, and what is it about those people that they are drawn to? All these things will help us understand our kids because, as they grow, they might end up having a different "why," or a different focus on mission, than you. But that's part of what parenting is all about—helping them to discover their own "why" and live it out.

FAMILY UNDER CONSTRUCTION

As I've been writing this book, Cheryl and I have prayed for those who will read it—that you will be inspired and equipped to raise a righteous brood aligned with the Spirit of the living God, who loves to make his home in your home.

You might be keen to start living missionally but feel like you don't know where to begin in the midst of busy family life. You might feel like there are too many hurdles to overcome. Maybe you feel you don't have enough space in your home.

Perhaps you're maxed-out with your job, or the "broken tree" part of your life is sapping all your emotional energy. Maybe you've realized you have some gaps in your own view of following Jesus. But I've shared how, as parents, it's our job to apprentice our kids in what we do. That means it has to start with us living it! Making the mission of God a family story needs to come from an overflow of our own lives and our own pursuit of God's vision and calling on us.

Whenever I notice a gap in my own life, I find it helps to act my way into thinking differently. Trying something actually changes the way we think—which then changes the way we act—which then changes the way we think. The first step might be that we, as parents, need to step out and really follow Jesus ourselves, taking some risks and going beyond just head knowledge.

Are there some areas where we need to repent of our desire and pursuit of a Metroville life rather than pursuing who Jesus calls us to be? Are there some things we need to stop doing, or give over to God, to ensure our hearts are wholly under his lordship? Do we need to start doing something that moves us toward the kingdom life God has called us to? You might feel apprehensive or have a whole load of reasons why it's not possible, but have a go at it.

Think back to before you had your first child. No doubt you tried to prepare everything before the baby was born: buying all the equipment, reading the baby books, packing the hospital bag. We think that if we just prepare well, we'll be ready and in control of this parenting thing. But of course, the reality is that when the baby comes along it's a complete whirlwind of feeding, changing diapers, burping, and bathing. Within a few days, all the carefully organized preparation has gone out the window—there are dirty diapers flowing out of the trashcan, and we're lucky if we've remembered to brush our teeth.

It's the same when we think about living missionally as a family. You don't have to get it all figured out before you begin. God's family is always under construction. There will never be a perfect time to step out into God's mission. Just as when you were new parents, you're going to learn a lot more on the job than in the preparation beforehand. Think about one thing you could do as a family to step into this kind of life together. Invite your kids to be part of shaping those steps.

So, make the holidays special for a handful that aren't in your immediate family. Have a spare room for those that need help. Love your neighbor as much as you love your own family! Create a home for the fatherless, the motherless, the orphans, the widows, and watch the family grow.

Invite your kids into a bigger story, a God story.

Here's to your righteous brood!

NOTES

1 COFFEE TIME

1   See Joe Carter, "Don't Blame the Pandemic for Low Church Attendance," *The Gospel Coalition*, January 29, 2022, https://www.thegospelcoalition.org/article/church-attendance-pandemic/.

2   "Atheism Doubles Among Generation Z," Barna, https://www.barna.com/research/atheism-doubles-among-generation-z/.

3   Isaiah 61:3.

4   See Acts 2:46b; Romans 16:5; 1 Corinthians 16:19; and Philemon 2.

5   See Matthew 5:13–16.

6   See, for example, John 3; Luke 8:1–3; Mark 10:46–52; John 8:1–11.

2 THE LURE OF METROVILLE

1   See Genesis 12.

2   See Matthew 1:1–17.

3   Karen Khachatryan, "Studying the Bible From Middle Eastern Perspective," Margins 2 Mic Episode 6, YouTube video, 21:56, https://thebroadcastnetwork.org/lessons/studying-the-bible-from-middle-eastern-perspective/.

4   Shaun Callaghan, Martin Lösch, Anna Pione, and Warren Teichner, "Feeling Good: The Future of the $1.5 Trillion Wellness Market," McKinsey & Company, April 8, 2021, https://www.

mckinsey.com/industries/consumer-packaged-goods/our-insights/
feeling-good-the-future-of-the-1-5-trillion-wellness-market.

5   Rami Gabriel, "How Do We Form Identities in a Consumer Society?"
Psychology Today, April 5, 2019,
https://www.psychologytoday.com/gb/blog/me-the-self-
and-i/201904/how-do-we-form-identities-in-consumer-society.

3 THE UPSIDE-DOWN KINGDOM

1   See "Gospel of the Kingdom," The Bible Project, https://bibleproject.
com/explore/video/gospel-kingdom/ for a great video resource on
the good news of the kingdom.

2   Matthew 5–7.

4 THE ALTAR: WHERE THE MISSIONAL FAMILY IS BORN

1   Genesis 12:1–3.

2   Read the full story in Genesis 22:1–18.

5 RAISING KINGDOMLINGS

1   See Romans 8:29.

2   See Matthew 5:17.

3   John 10:10.

4   Colossians 3:21.

5   See Jeremiah 17:9 and Matthew 15:19, for example.

6   Hebrews 10:16.

7   Emily Perlman Abedon, "Toddler Empathy," Parents.com,
October 3, 2005, https://www.parents.com/toddlers-preschoolers/
development/behavioral/toddler-empathy/.

8   Luke 15:11–32.

6   FINDING YOUR GROOVE

1   Luke 5:29.

2   John 2:1–12.

3   Luke 22:7–23.

4   Luke 10:6.

5   Matthew 22:37–39.

6   See, for example, "The Learning Pyramid," The Peak Performance Center, https://thepeakperformancecenter.com/educational-learning/learning/principles-of-learning/learning-pyramid/.

7   See Ken Ham, "Barna: The Pandemic Will Accelerate Young People Leaving the Church," *Answers in Genesis*, October 28, 2020, https://answersingenesis.org/church/barna-pandemic-will-accelerate-young-people-leaving-church/.

8   See Mark 1:14–15.

9   Luke 4:18–19.

10 Matthew 16:18.

7   BROKEN TREES

1   "2012 Disability Status Report–Colorado," Cornell University, https://www.disabilitystatistics.org/StatusReports/2012-PDF/2012-StatusReport_CO.pdf.

2   John 10:10.

3   See 1 Samuel 23 for more on David's mighty men.

ACKNOWLEDGMENTS

First, and most obviously, I thank Cheryl and our kids—Alli, Mckenna, and our late son, Ryan—for being the ones I have gotten to do my life with and for. The crazy ride isn't over! I also want to give a shout out to my two sons-in-law, Matthew and Jessie, for taking on my daughters and continuing the legacy of crazy living and real faith. And to the littles—Mila, Leo, Ezekiel, K and D—we have hopes and dreams for you all, and we can't wait to watch as you find true faith and follow God's paths for you.

I also want to thank some unique families around the world who we've spent significant time with and who in special ways inspired us not to be normal. To the Grafs, the Colons, the Iskarous, the McCalls, the Kramers, and the Hirsches—for making a family out of anyone you found on your front porch. Thank you for showing us new ways to be a family living out God's story.

ABOUT THE AUTHOR

Hugh Halter and his wife, Cheryl, have been missionaries in North America for more than thirty years. They've planted two churches and in 2016 founded Lantern Network in Alton, Illinois. Lantern Network is a kingdom ecosystem committed to incubating good works and benevolent businesses to bless the city. Hugh speaks extensively across the globe, encouraging innovative forms of church, and when home loves to help Cheryl run Rí Beag Refuge, an eighty-acre equine therapy farm. Hugh is a leading missional voice, authoring such books as *The Tangible Kingdom*, *AND: The Gathered and Scattered Church*, *Flesh*, and, more recently, the Life as Mission Series, which seeks to equip Christians to live the missionary life of Jesus in their everyday context. Look out for future offerings from the Life as Mission Series!

Life as Mission Series

Resources that equip Christians to live the missionary life of Jesus in their everyday context.

Look out for other offerings in the Life as Mission Series.
Go to **lifeasmission.co**

Made in United States
Troutdale, OR
10/17/2023

13782986R00116